100 MOST DANGEROUS THINGS ON THE PLANET

Published by Scholastic Australia Pty Limited
PO Box 579, Gosford NSW 2250
ABN 11 000 614 577

Part of the Scholastic Group
Sydney • Auckland • New York • Toronto • London • Mexico City
New Delhi • Hong Kong • Buenos Aires • Puerto Rico

Conceived, edited, and designed by Marshall Editions
The Old Brewery
6 Blundell Street
London N7 9BH

Publisher: Dominic Carman
Art director: Ivo Marloh
Managing editor: Paul Docherty
Project editor: Deborah Hercun
Design: Claire Harvey
Layout: 3rd-I
Production: Nikki Ingram
Picture research: Veneta Bullen

This edition published by Scholastic Australia in 2008
Copyright © 2008 Marshall Editions

ISBN: 978-1-74169-142-9

Printed and bound in China by SNP Leefung Printers Ltd

10 9 8 7 6 5 4 3 2 1

First printing 2008

Cover: tl Corbis/Theo Allofs; tr Science Photo Library/Fred K Smith; b Quarto

Anna Claybourne

100 MOST DANGEROUS THINGS ON THE PLANET

CONTENTS

Human Dangers

INTRODUCTION

Today the world is probably safer for humans than it has ever been. Modern medicines, emergency services, warm dry houses, and clean water supplies have saved millions of lives. That's why, in most countries, the population is rising, and people are living longer and longer.

WILD WORLD

However, there are still some dangers that we can do little about. Human technology is no match for the mighty power of an exploding volcano or the force of a 30-metre- (100-foot-) high tsunami, or a powerful tornado. And much of our world is made up of remote wilderness and ocean, where you can easily get lost, or find yourself face-to-face with a dangerous animal.

LOOK AFTER YOURSELF

Of course, the best way to stay safe is to avoid dangerous situations in the first place.

STAY AWAY

Don't explore wild places alone, or without the right equipment. Whenever you can, keep clear of the kinds of dangerous things described in this book, such as thin ice, poisonous animals, or avalanche-risk areas.

WARNING

This book contains the most useful advice available for various dangerous situations. But the tips here are only general guidelines, and cannot be guaranteed to keep you safe. In a dangerous situation, there may be no truly safe option.

USE COMMON SENSE

Never do dangerous things for a laugh or a dare. If you don't feel safe, or you know something is risky, don't do it. If other people are doing it, try to persuade them not to, or get help.

HEED WARNINGS

In many dangerous places, such as crumbling cliffs and beaches with strong currents, there are signs to warn you where it's not safe to go. They are there to help you – don't ignore them!

OBEY INSTRUCTIONS

This book contains useful tips for lots of different kinds of dangers. But in a *particular* situation, such as an earthquake in your area, or seeing a dangerous animal, you should follow any instructions given to you by local guides, emergency services, or local warning systems. They are more likely to know the best course of action for that particular event.

On February 22, 1999, two large avalanches hit the town of Evolene in the Swiss Alps. Twelve people were killed, and more than a dozen went missing.

RISK RATING

☠	Rare
☠ ☠	Unlikely
☠ ☠ ☠	Likely
☠ ☠ ☠ ☠	Very Likely
☠ ☠ ☠ ☠ ☠	Frequent

DID YOU KNOW?

- A lightning bolt can be 6 times hotter than the surface of the Sun
- Hippos kill far more people than sharks do
- One of the biggest dangers in deserts is the cold – the temperature can be freezing at night

READ ON TO FIND OUT MORE...

NATURAL

Much of our planet is wild and full of natural dangers. You could get lost in one of the world's vast deserts, jungles, oceans, or icy polar regions, or you could encounter a dangerous animal such as

DANGERS

a deadly snake, spider, or jellyfish. Natural disasters such as earthquakes and tsunamis, and violent weather such as tornadoes and lightning, can affect us even when we're at home.

VOLCANIC ERUPTION

When a volcano erupts, hot lava (melted rock), gas, and burning ash burst out from inside Earth. An eruption can fling solid rock into the air, too. Most volcanoes have erupted many times before, forming mountains. They are closely monitored, so if one is about to erupt, there will usually be lots of warnings. But people do sometimes get caught in an eruption.

DANGER RATING

RISK RATING: ☠ ☠ ☠
Millions of people live close to volcanoes, but there are only around 60 eruptions a year.

SURVIVAL RATING: 80%
You should be able to escape, even if you're on the volcano.

WHAT TO DO

IF THERE'S A WARNING:
The local area will be evacuated. Follow instructions and leave the area as quickly and safely as possible. Take blankets, food, and water in case you get stuck.

IF A VOLCANO ERUPTS NEAR YOU:
Head for high ground to avoid lava and mud that may flow down valleys. Wear clothes that protect you from falling ash. Protect your eyes with goggles, and your mouth and nose with a wet cloth.

IF A VOLCANO ERUPTS WHILE YOU'RE ON IT:
Head for a high ridge on the mountainside and avoid valleys, streams, and bridges. Look for large rocks for shelter.

TOP TIP! If rocks start falling around you, curl up and cover your head!

LAVA FLOW

Some volcanoes erupt very gently and quietly. There's no big explosion — just lava flowing down the volcano's sides. It could take you by surprise if it suddenly flows faster or changes direction.

You can even have a lava flow without a volcano. Sometimes lava comes to the surface of Earth's crust in an unexpected place, forming a new volcano.

WHAT TO DO

IF A LAVA FLOW IS COMING:

If you see lava heading your way, move quickly, heading uphill. Check for other lava flows as you go, so that you don't get trapped. Steer clear of water and plants, as lava can explode when it touches them.

IF LAVA SURROUNDS YOU:

You need to get away fast, while the flow is small. Jump over it if you can do so safely. Or look out for rocks you can use as stepping stones. Avoid stepping on fresh lava, even if it looks solid.

AVOID LAVA BURNS:

Near lava, wear tough leather boots, long sleeves and trousers, a hat, gloves, and sunglasses or goggles. If lava spatters or explodes, turn your face away quickly to avoid burns.

HOW HOT?

Lava is VERY HOT. It is made of melted rock — and it takes very high temperatures to melt rock. Most lava is at least 500°C (930°F), but it can be as hot as 1,300°C (2,370°F).

Kilauea Volcano in Hawaii is one of many volcanoes around the world where visitors can watch lava flows in action.

DANGER RATING

RISK RATING: ☠ ☠ ☠
Lava is a danger to the many tourists who visit active volcanoes.

SURVIVAL RATING: 90%
As most lava is slow-moving, you can usually get away from it.

PYROCLASTIC FLOW

A pyroclastic flow is one of the most dangerous and deadly of all volcanic events. It is a mixture of hot gas, rocks, and ash that surges downhill from an erupting volcano. It moves fast, like a flowing river. In fact, pyroclastic flows can reach speeds of 160 kph (100 mph) and can be as hot as 700°C (1,300°F). You do NOT want to be caught up in one!

WHAT TO DO

IF A PYROCLASTIC FLOW IS COMING:

You can't move fast enough to outrun a pyroclastic flow, even in a car. Instead, try to see where it's heading and get out of the way. Move to the side and away from low ground.

IF YOU'RE IN THE WAY:

If a pyroclastic flow lands on you, it's too late! But if you're near the edge of the flow, you could survive. Hide behind a rock, or in any shelter you can find, such as a hut. As the flow passes, cover your head and hold your breath. Breathing in the hot gas, dust, and ash will destroy your lungs.

DANGER RATING

RISK RATING: ☠

Pyroclastic flows are very rare, occuring only a few times a year.

SURVIVAL RATING: 10%

Your only chance of survival is to avoid the path of the flow.

DID YOU KNOW?

The ancient Italian town of Pompeii was flattened by a pyroclastic flow from the volcano Vesuvius in AD 79. The ash hardened around the victims' bodies, forming human-shaped spaces.

MUDFLOW OR LAHAR

A volcanic mudflow, or lahar, happens when volcanic ash mixes with water. The water can come from heavy rain, from a lake or river, or a volcanic eruption melting snow and ice. The mixture forms fast-flowing mud that can rush down a volcano's valleys and drown whole towns. Like a river, a lahar can travel a long way from the eruption itself.

WHAT TO DO

IF THERE'S A WARNING:
Many areas at risk of mudflows have warning systems in place. Obey the instructions and move away from valleys and rivers to high ground as fast as you can.

IF A MUDFLOW STRIKES:
If you're caught in a lahar, you'll be safer the higher up you are. Go inside a tall, strong building and go upstairs. If there's no building, climbing a large tree could save your life.

TRAPPED IN THE MUD:
Try to keep your head above the mud and cling on to floating objects as you wait for rescue.

DANGER RATING

RISK RATING: ☠ ☠
There's almost always a risk of mudflows when a volcano erupts.

SURVIVAL RATING: 90%
Mudflows have been big killers in the past, but today's satellite technology can usually see them coming.

MUDFLOW HORROR

In 1985, a lahar from the Nevado del Ruiz volcano in Colombia drowned the town of Armero, killing over 23,000 people. If they had known it was coming, the townspeople could have climbed to nearby high ground and escaped.

SUPERVOLCANO

A supervolcano is a huge volcanic eruption, far bigger than a normal volcano. As a normal volcano erupts, lava cools and builds up around it, making a mountain. But a supervolcano throws so much lava and rock out of the ground that it leaves a bowl-shaped crater, or caldera.

There were several supervolcanic eruptions in prehistoric times. For example, Yellowstone National Park in the USA is on the site of an old supervolcano, which might one day erupt again.

WHAT TO DO

IF A SUPERVOLCANO IS PREDICTED:
If there's time, the area around the supervolcano will be evacuated. Leave quickly, but stay calm to avoid travel chaos.

DURING THE ERUPTION:
If you're more than 100 kilometres (60 miles) from the eruption, you could survive. A heavy ash fall will cover the land for thousands of kilometres in every direction. Stay indoors to shelter from it – don't try to drive through it.

AFTER THE EVENT:
Ash thrown into orbit will surround Earth and blot out sunlight, making it hard to grow crops. You may be able to survive on stockpiled, preserved foods.

DANGER RATING

RISK RATING: ☠
A supervolcano will erupt again, but we do not know when.

SURVIVAL RATING: 50%
A big supervolcano would destroy a huge area, and many people would die.

TOP TIP! Don't panic! There's so little we can do about a supervolcano, there's no point worrying about it.

AVALANCHE

An avalanche happens when a big pile of snow slips down a mountainside. Many things can cause avalanches – wind, sunshine melting the snow, snowmobiles or skiers dislodging it, or new snow piling up into an unstable heap.

Avalanches can be deadly if the snow buries people or houses. It is heavy and hard to dig through, and people often run out of air before rescuers can reach them.

DANGER RATING

RISK RATING: ☠ ☠ ☠
Avalanches happen every year, often in popular ski resorts.

SURVIVAL RATING: 60%
You can survive if you can avoid the path of the avalanche or dig your way out.

HI-TECH HELP

Many skiers now carry an avalanche transceiver. This gadget gives out a radio signal that lets rescuers locate them if they are buried by an avalanche.

WHAT TO DO

IF YOU SEE AN AVALANCHE:

Move sideways to try to avoid the avalanche. Try to take shelter behind a large rock or hold on to a tree and try to stay upright.

IF YOU'RE SWEPT AWAY:

Drop your backpack, as it will weigh you down. Make swimming movements to try to stay on the surface of the snow.

IF YOU'RE BURIED IN THE SNOW:

Curl into a ball, with your hands in front of your face to make a space for air. Spit into your hands – the spit will fall downwards, telling you the other way is up. Dig upwards with your hands or a ski pole before the snow hardens.

EARTHQUAKE

Earth's crust (surface layer) is made up of several large sections, called tectonic plates. They slowly move around, squeezing and grinding against one another. Sometimes, they catch one another, and the tension builds up until the plates suddenly slip. The ground jerks and trembles in an earthquake. Big earthquakes can tear cracks in the ground, causing buildings to collapse.

During a massive earthquake in 1995 a freeway collapsed in Kobe, Japan.

WHAT TO DO

EARTHQUAKE WARNING:
It's hard for scientists to predict earthquakes, but they sometimes can. It may be possible to evacuate the area in time. If an earthquake is coming, prepare. Put heavy objects on the floor. Collect plenty of water in buckets and bottles. Put out any fires and flames safely.

DURING AN EARTHQUAKE:
If you're indoors, shelter in a doorway or under a heavy table or desk. Stay away from the kitchen, stairways, lifts, and windows.

DANGER RATING

RISK RATING: ☠ ☠ ☠
There are dozens of major earthquakes around the world each year.

SURVIVAL RATING: 80%
Earthquakes can be disastrous, but in most cases, many people survive the event.

If you're outdoors, move away from houses, trees, power lines, bridges, and other things that could fall on you.

TOP TIP! After an earthquake, there could be another quake, or smaller shakes called tremors. Don't assume the quake is over – avoid danger while you wait for rescue.

RISK RATING: ☠ ☠
A sinkhole opening under your house or street is very unlikely.

SURVIVAL RATING: 60%
You may survive falling into a sinkhole, or be able to run away before you do.

This sinkhole appeared in Guatemala City, Guatemala, in 2007. It swallowed 12 houses and killed three people.

SINKHOLE

Imagine a huge hole in the ground suddenly opening up right under your feet! A sinkhole is simply a hole in the ground, caused by water wearing away underground rocks. Many sinkholes form gradually. But sometimes, water hollows out an invisible underground chamber, covered by a thin layer of rock. Eventually this "roof" collapses inwards, and a gaping hole appears. If this happens in a busy, built-up area, it can be disastrous.

WHAT TO DO

SPOT A SINKHOLE:
Sinkholes can appear without warning. Sometimes, though, there are warning signs, such as a circular pattern of cracks in the ground, earth tremors, and a deep rumbling noise. If these things happen, leave the area and call the emergency services.

IF A SINKHOLE APPEARS:
If the ground starts to sink, run uphill towards the edge of the sinkhole. Hold on to railings or other fixed objects to pull yourself up.

IF YOU FALL IN:
You might land in water, which will break your fall. Tread water, cling to floating objects, and yell!

DID YOU KNOW?

Sometimes, a sinkhole opens up at the bottom of a lake. The lake disappears into it, like bath water going down the drain.

TSUNAMI

Tourists and locals run for their lives from the massive Indian Ocean tsunami of 2004.

A tsunami is a giant wave or series of waves that crash onto the shore, usually because of an undersea earthquake. As a tsunami nears the shore, it builds up into a wall of water, which can reach heights of 10–30 metres (30–100 feet). The force of the water can destroy everything in its path.

DANGER RATING

RISK RATING: ☠ ☠ ☠
There are several large tsunamis each year around the world. Being caught in one is unlikely, but when they strike they can kill thousands.

SURVIVAL RATING: 70%
If a tsunami strikes a town or village, it will almost certainly be a killer. But you have a good chance of survival if you know what to do.

WHAT TO DO

IF A TSUNAMI IS COMING:
Head inland as fast as you can and aim for high ground. Try to get to the top of a tall hill. Alternatively, go inside the biggest, strongest building you can see and make for an upper floor.

IF THE WAVE IS ABOUT TO HIT YOU:
Climb a tree or grab hold of a fixed object such as a railing or parking meter. Use your clothes to tie yourself to it, and try to cling on as the tsunami passes.

IF IT WASHES YOU AWAY:
Look for a floating object to hold on to, and try to protect your head. Yell for help.

WARNING SIGNS:
These signs can sometimes tell you a tsunami is on the way:
• You feel an earthquake when you're close to the shore.
• The sea suddenly becomes rough and boats bob up and down.
• The sea is quickly sucked away from the beach, leaving the seabed bare.

TOP TIP! Some areas, especially around the Pacific where tsunamis are most common, have signs showing you where to go if one is coming.

TSUNAMI HAZARD ZONE
IN CASE OF EARTHQUAKE, G[O]
TO HIGH GROUND OR INLAN[D]

ASTEROID STRIKE

An asteroid is a lump of rock zooming through space. Most are far away from Earth, but sometimes one comes so close to Earth that gravity sucks it in, and it falls to the ground.

A big asteroid strike could have devastating results. It would flatten the area it landed on, blow out a huge crater, and trigger tsunamis. It could also fill the sky with debris, blocking out the sunlight.

DANGER RATING

RISK RATING: ☠
The chance of an asteroid landing on you is tiny.

SURVIVAL RATING: 50%
It depends on the asteroid – a small one might not harm anyone, but a big one could wipe out life on Earth.

WHAT TO DO

IF AN ASTEROID
IS COMING:
Scientists should be able to predict a strike, giving time to warn the public. The likely landing site would be evacuated. It would be wise to stockpile food and water. People on the coast should head for high ground, in case of tsunamis.

IF IT'S ABOUT TO LAND:
If an asteroid hits you, you'll have no chance. But if it's far away, you could survive. Shelter from the initial blast under doorways or heavy furniture.

AFTER THE IMPACT:
Stay indoors to hide from falling debris. Later, you may be able to travel to a safer area.

Asteroids range from pea-sized to many kilometres wide. An asteroid 10 m (33 ft) across could destroy a town. An asteroid 100 m (330 ft) across could destroy an area the size of Britain. An asteroid 10 km (6 miles) across could wipe out the human race.

DID YOU KNOW? Scientists are working on ways to deflect asteroids that come too close. One idea is firing a rocket at an asteroid to make it change direction and miss Earth.

FREAK WAVE

This computer-generated image shows the awesome scale of a freak wave.

DANGER RATING

RISK RATING: ☠
Freak waves are rare, and it's even rarer that they hit a boat.
SURVIVAL RATING: 70%
If the wave doesn't sink your boat in seconds, you'll probably escape its worst effects.

A freak, or rogue, wave is a giant wave that appears far out at sea. It is not a tsunami or a storm wave. It's a sea wave that is much bigger and steeper than normal. The biggest storm waves are about 15 metres (50 feet) high, but a freak wave can reach 25 metres (80 feet) or even 30 metres (100 feet) high. Freak waves may lie behind many unexplained sinkings.

Experts think freak waves can be caused by wind, currents, or by several waves joining together, but they are not sure.

DID YOU KNOW?

Sailors have been reporting freak waves for centuries, but many people thought they were just exaggerated tales. In 2003, scientists proved freak waves existed by using satellites in space to detect them.

WHAT TO DO

IF YOU SEE A FREAK WAVE:
If you're on a ship and you see a freak wave, get indoors fast. Move to the other side of the ship, away from the wave. Stay away from windows. Find something to hold on to and hang on tight.

IF THE WAVE CRASHES OVER YOU:
If you're on deck when the wave comes, your only chance is to grab something fixed, such as a railing, and hang on to it. Put your head down and hold your breath as the wave passes.

AVOIDING FREAK WAVES:
Scientists are trying to calculate where in the world freak waves happen most, and working on early warning systems to help boats avoid freak wave disasters.

ICEBERG

The word "iceberg" means "ice mountain". An iceberg is a huge, floating chunk of ice that has broken off from a glacier. Icebergs form around the Arctic and Antarctic, where glaciers (slow rivers of ice) flow into the sea and break up.

Ice is slightly lighter than water. This means that icebergs float – but only just. As an iceberg drifts, only about 12 per cent is visible above the surface; the rest is underwater. The rock-hard ice can cause disaster if a ship hits it.

WHAT TO DO

IF YOU SEE AN ICEBERG:
All kinds of boats should stay away from icebergs. Even if it looks far away, part of the iceberg could be just under the water nearby. Never go closer to get a better look. Icebergs can suddenly roll over or shed big lumps of ice, creating dangerous waves.

IF YOU HIT AN ICEBERG:
An iceberg can rip a boat open under the waterline. If you're on a big ship, such as a cruiser, go to an upper deck and follow any instructions from the captain and crew.

This cross section picture shows how much of an iceberg is underwater.

DANGER RATING

RISK RATING: ☠ ☠ ☠
There are thousands of icebergs floating around. They are a constant danger to ships, undersea cables, and oil rigs.

SURVIVAL RATING: 80%
As icebergs move slowly, it's usually possible to avoid them.

THE TITANIC

An iceberg caused one of the most famous disasters in history – the sinking of the *Titanic* in 1912. People said the new ocean liner was unsinkable, but she hit an iceberg and sank within hours. There were not enough lifeboats, and around 1,500 people died.

FLOOD

A flood happens when water overflows an area of land. Many rivers flood the land around them every year without causing problems, because people know what to expect. But sudden, unexpected flooding can be much more serious. It can be caused by heavy rainfall, or by the sea overflowing the land because of a sea storm or tsunami.

Floodwater can sweep away people, cars, and houses, or cause damage by spreading mud and sewage far and wide.

A man wearing garbage bags on his legs struggles through the floodwaters in Venice.

WHAT TO DO

IF THERE'S A FLOOD WARNING:

Leave the area and go to stay somewhere safer. Make sure pets are safe, too. Move valuable and electrical items upstairs or put them high up. Switch off the gas and electricity supply, and if you have them, pile sandbags around your home. If you are staying, store fresh water, food, a first aid kit, torches, and blankets.

IF YOU'RE CUT OFF BY FLOODWATER:

Stay calm! Try to contact the emergency services using a mobile phone if possible.

DANGER RATING

RISK RATING: ☠ ☠ ☠ ☠
Floods happen all around the world every year, and they are becoming more common.
SURVIVAL RATING: 90%
Though floods can be very dangerous, they usually cause more damage to property than to people.

Otherwise, wave or shine a torch at passing boats or helicopters. Keep any food and water supplies safe. Don't try to escape through the water – wait to be rescued.

IF YOU'RE SWEPT AWAY:

Cling to floating objects and try to grab on to a tree or signpost. Yell and wave to help rescuers see you.

FLASH FLOOD

Flash floods are floods that occur suddenly. Usually, a flash flood is caused by a thunderstorm dropping a lot of heavy rain in a short time. It can collect into a torrent of water that surges down narrow river valleys. A dam collapsing can also cause a flash flood.

Flash floods are dangerous because they take people by surprise. They often happen in summer, when rivers are calm and people are enjoying fishing, hiking, or swimming there.

Hurricane Dean caused severe flash floods in August 2007 in Dominica.

WHAT TO DO

IF YOU SEE OR HEAR A FLASH FLOOD COMING:
If you're in a valley, you may spot a flash flood upriver, or hear a loud roaring sound. Move fast – climb up the sides of the valley, away from the water. As the flood approaches, look for a tree to hold on to.

IF YOU'RE SWEPT AWAY:
Try to tread water or hold on to a floating branch, and swim for the bank. If you can, grab a tree on the bank and hold on.

AVOID FLASH FLOODS:
Flash floods are hard to predict, but think twice before visiting a deep valley or gorge if you know heavy rain is forecast.

DID YOU KNOW?
Many of the victims of flash floods die not from drowning, but from being hit by the rocks, branches, and logs carried along by the powerful surging water.

LANDSLIDE

In June 2005 a massive landslide in Laguna Beach, California, sent 18 homes crashing down a hill.

DANGER RATING

RISK RATING: ☠ ☠ ☠
Landslides are fairly common, though most are quite small.

SURVIVAL RATING: 80%
Most landslides don't fall on people, and even when they do, some survive.

A landslide is just what it sounds like – a section of land sliding downhill. They can happen on steep slopes or cliffs when the ground is soaked by heavy rain or melting snow, making the soil heavy and slippery. Earthquakes and volcanic eruptions can also trigger landslides. A landslide can cause a disaster if the rock and soil falls on houses, or if it falls into water, causing a tsunami.

WHAT TO DO

LOOK OUT FOR LANDSLIDES:

You can sometimes tell that a landslide is about to happen. You might see small trickles of soil flowing downhill, and trees might start to tilt as the earth shifts. Stream water may turn muddy. If you see these signs, call the emergency services and leave the area, warning neighbours too.

DURING A LANDSLIDE:

If there's time, head sideways out of the path of the landslide. Don't try to take anything with you – drop everything and run. If the landslide is going to fall on you, curl into a ball with your arms around your head. If you're indoors, shelter under heavy furniture. Outdoors, hide behind a big rock or tree.

DAM DISASTER

In 1963, a landslide plunged into a reservoir behind the Vaiont Dam in Italy. It created a huge wave, which flowed over the dam and onto several villages below, killing 2,000 people.

SOLAR FLARE

Our sun is a giant ball of very hot, burning gas. On its surface are cooler areas known as sunspots. Sometimes, near a sunspot, a massive explosion of energy bursts out from the sun. This is a solar flare. It flings out huge amounts of radiation, such as X-rays, into space. If these rays are thrown towards Earth, they can damage electronic equipment, such as space satellites. If a really big solar flare hit Earth, experts think it might destroy electrical systems and cause a major disaster.

DANGER RATING

RISK RATING: ☠
Solar flares happen regularly, but one big enough to cause disaster is not very likely.

SURVIVAL RATING: 50%
A really huge solar flare could lead to devastation on Earth.

WHAT TO DO

DON'T WORRY:
We can't control the sun, so there's nothing we can do to stop a massive solar flare. And if it affects the whole Earth, there's nowhere to escape to anyway. It is also very unlikely.

IF IT HAPPENS:
A giant solar flare might cut off electricity and communications systems. This would bring the world to a standstill – things like banks, transport systems, GPS networks, phones, and computers would stop working. The best preparation for this is to have good basic survival skills and equipment, such as torches, tools, and first aid knowledge.

DID YOU KNOW? Sunspots and solar flares follow a regular cycle. Every 11 years or so, they reach maximum strength, then calm down again. The next peak is due around 2011.

LAKE OVERTURN

When you open a fizzy drink bottle, bubbles zoom up to the top. The same thing can happen in a lake. Some lakes form over volcanic vents, which release gases into the water. If the lake is deep, the water at the bottom is under great pressure. The gas dissolves in the deep water, and the water above holds it down.

But if something disturbs the lake, such as an earth tremor, the gas-filled water can rise to the surface. The gas escapes in what is known as a limnic eruption, or a lake overturn. It rolls out of the lake in a huge cloud that can suffocate people and animals.

LAKE NYOS The deadliest lake overturn on record happened at Lake Nyos in Cameroon, Africa, in 1986. It killed about 1,700 people and thousands of cattle.

WHAT TO DO

IF YOU SEE BUBBLES FORMING:
If you see lake water starting to fizz and bubble, it could be the start of a lake overturn. Head uphill from the lake and raise the alarm.

IF YOU'RE CAUGHT IN A GAS CLOUD:
The gas in a lake overturn is usually carbon dioxide. It is heavier than air, so it flows downhill into valleys. To escape, move uphill, away from valleys and low areas.

PREVENTING LAKE OVERTURNS:
Scientists are trying to prevent lake overturns by installing pipes in some volcanic lakes. The pipe lets gas escape from the depths of the lake at a slow, safe rate.

SEICHE

"Seiche" is a French word that means "sway". During a seiche, the water in a lake, bay, or pond sways or sloshes to and fro. First it rises up at one end of the lake, and down at the other. Then it sloshes back the other way. As the water rocks back and forth, it can overflow onto the land, sweeping people away and causing floods.

Seiches are usually caused by storms and strong winds pushing at the lake surface. Earthquakes and volcanic eruptions can sometimes cause seiches, too.

The Great Lakes of Canada and the USA have seiches, known locally as sloshes, on a regular basis. Lake Erie is particularly affected because of its long shape and shallow water.

WHAT TO DO

SEICHE WARNING:
On lakes that have regular seiches, such as Lake Michigan in the USA, there are warnings when a seiche is likely. Avoid the lake shore, don't go out in a boat, and keep away from piers.

DURING A SEICHE:
In a seiche, water can rise up suddenly and wash over the shore. If you see it coming, run inland or get inside a building. If you are washed away, stay calm. Try to swim towards the shore and cling on to railings, a tree, or other fixed object until the water subsides.

DANGER RATING

RISK RATING: ☠ ☠
Seiches are fairly rare, and most of them are quite small.

SURVIVAL RATING: 90%
Seiches can be killers, but there is usually a warning. Most seiches are not big like tsunamis.

A seiche works just like water sloshing to and fro in a bathtub.

DID YOU KNOW?
Seiches can happen in swimming pools – especially after an earthquake. If you're swimming when an earthquake happens, get out of the water.

WILDFIRE

When fire sweeps through forests, fields, or outback, it's called a wildfire or bushfire. Most wildfires happen in summer and fall, when trees and grass have dried out and catch fire easily. Wind can fan the flames and help the fire spread. Wildfires destroy thousands of trees and plants. Sometimes, they burn down houses or trap people in their cars.

Some wildfires start naturally, sparked by lightning or a volcanic eruption. Others are caused by people making campfires, dropping cigarettes, or even starting a fire on purpose to cause damage.

DANGER RATING

RISK RATING: ☠ ☠ ☠
Wildfires are a serious danger in many parts of the world, and hundreds happen every year.

SURVIVAL RATING: 80%
Being caught in a wildfire is very dangerous, but people usually manage to get away.

WHAT TO DO

IF THERE'S A WILDFIRE WARNING:

Check radio and TV broadcasts for evacuation instructions. Plan an escape route and talk to your neighbours – if your family has a car, you could arrange to take someone who doesn't. Find your pets and have them ready to go. Put important documents and emergency supplies in the car, which should be ready with the keys in the ignition.

IF A WILDFIRE IS CLOSING IN:

If you're at home, use a hose to wet the roof, walls, and surroundings. If you're on the move, check the direction of the smoke and flames to see where the fire is going, and head another way. If the fire is about to catch you, you'll be safest in water. Look for a river or lake that you can get into safely.

TOP TIP! You can help to prevent wildfires. Don't start campfires in the wild, and always take all your litter home with you.

FIRESTORM

DANGER RATING

RISK RATING: ☠
Only a few wildfires lead to a firestorm.

SURVIVAL RATING: 60%
Firestorms are hotter, more powerful, and more dangerous than a regular wildfire.

A firestorm is a very intense, dangerous kind of wildfire that creates a fiery windstorm. As a fire burns, it causes an updraft. The hot air rises upwards, and cooler air is sucked inwards to replace it. If the fire is very intense, this effect can create powerful whirlwinds and even lightning. In turn, the winds fan the flames, making the fire far hotter than a normal wildfire. As well as spreading the fire, firestorm winds fill the air with smoke, making it hard to see.

WHAT TO DO

SPOT A FIRESTORM:
Signs of a firestorm include the noise of the fire getting quieter at first, then much louder. You may see a mushroom-shaped cloud of smoke above the fire, and feel the air getting very hot, even from some distance away.

In the summer of 2007, fires raged across large parts of Greece. Here a firefighting airplane battles a firestorm in the forest of Mount Hymettus, on the edge of Athens.

GET AWAY:
If you see a firestorm, don't stick around. Move away from it quickly, in a car if possible. Don't stop to stare at it!

IF YOU ARE TRAPPED:
If the firestorm is on top of you, your only chance is to get into water, or get down as low as you can. Inside a house, shut yourself in the basement. In a forest, try to crawl away from the fire, covering your face with your clothes.

DID YOU KNOW?
Firestorms can also happen during fires in cities. The Great Fire of London, which destroyed most of the city in 1666, is thought to have involved a firestorm.

HURRICANE

Hurricane Georges battering the coast of Puerto Rico in September 1998.

DANGER RATING

RISK RATING:

Big hurricanes happen every year, and experts think they are becoming more common as Earth gets warmer.

SURVIVAL RATING: 90%

Hurricanes can be deadly, but as there's plenty of warning, most people survive.

Hurricanes are the world's biggest storms. They form over the ocean, when warm weather makes hot, damp air rise upwards. This sucks in more air, which spins around and around, building a giant spiral of swirling rain clouds.

A hurricane can be 500 kilometres (300 miles) across, with wind speeds reaching 290 kph (180 mph). Usually, hurricanes move slowly across the sea until they meet land. There they can cause great devastation.

WHAT TO DO

WHEN A HURRICANE COMES:
Scientists can track hurricanes at sea using satellites, so they usually know when one is coming. If you are told to evacuate the area, fill your car with petrol, pack emergency food, water, medicines, and blankets, and head inland. If there's time, protect your home. Move all outdoor furniture and objects inside. If you don't have window shutters, fix plywood boards over the windows.

DURING A HURRICANE:
You'll be safest indoors. Stay in the middle of the building you are in, away from windows. If you're outdoors, look for any kind of shelter. Don't hide under a bridge, though, as the wind may speed up there. Keep away from floodwater, and avoid power lines as they could fall on you.

TOP TIP! If the weather suddenly goes calm and quiet, don't think it's all over! It's probably just the "eye" of the hurricane – the small calm area in the middle of the storm. Stay where you are until the rest of the hurricane has passed by.

TORNADO

A tornado is smaller than a hurricane, but its winds can be even faster – up to 500 kph (300 mph). Tornadoes form during thunderstorms, when a column of air moves downwards from a thundercloud. More air spirals around it, forming a cone-shaped funnel of wind. Most tornadoes look dark because their strong winds pick up dust, rubble, and debris. Tornadoes can cause devastation, flattening homes and flinging cars around as they track across the land.

WHAT TO DO

IF A TORNADO IS COMING:
If you spot a tornado, get indoors and hide in a basement, or in a downstairs room in the middle of the house. Shelter under a heavy table and put cushions or blankets around it to catch flying objects. Mobile homes are not safe. If you're in one, leave it and shelter in a solid building, or a purpose-built tornado shelter.

IF YOU'RE OUTDOORS:
If you're in a car, get out of it and run for shelter. Tornadoes can lift cars high into the air, then drop them. If there's no building to shelter in, lie down in a ditch and cover your head.

SKY SIGN You can sometimes tell when a tornado is about to form, because the sky turns a strange dark green colour!

A killer tornado tears up southern Maryland, USA, in April 2002. Wind speeds reached up to 509 kph (318 mph), killing two people and injuring 95 in the devastated town of La Plata.

BLIZZARD

A blizzard is a severe snowstorm in which heavy snowfall combines with swirling winds. The snow whirls around and fills the air, making it very hard to see where you are going. Meanwhile, snowdrifts collect on the ground, making driving and walking almost impossible. Being caught outdoors in a blizzard is very dangerous.

DANGER RATING

RISK RATING: ☠ ☠

Serious blizzards are fairly rare, and there's usually time to reach safety.

SURVIVAL RATING: 80%

You should be safe in a blizzard as long as you find shelter fast.

WHAT TO DO

IN BLIZZARD CONDITIONS: Stay at home, or shelter in a shop or another warm building as soon as you can. It's a good idea to leave some lights on in case someone else is lost in the blizzard and searching for shelter.

IF YOU'RE IN A CAR: Make sure the car is pulled over in a safe place as soon as possible. Call for help using a mobile phone, and switch on the lights to help emergency services find you. While you're waiting, wrap up in coats, hats, blankets, and any other coverings you can find.

IF YOU'RE ON FOOT: Call for help on a mobile phone if possible. Look out for lights that could show you where a house is, or use any kind of shelter you can find, like a bus shelter, cave, or phone booth. Wear all the clothes you have with you, and keep your hands and head covered to ward off frostbite.

A snowplough lies crashed in Slovakia after the region was hit by heavy snowstorms in 2005.

FROSTBITE

Frostbite is a danger in snow and ice storms. It happens when blood vessels freeze in a body part such as your fingers, toes, or nose. The affected part goes black, and may have to be cut off.

ICE STORM

DANGER RATING

RISK RATING: ☠

Ice storms mainly happen in the USA and Canada. It is a rare event in the UK.

SURVIVAL RATING: 95%

Usually, most of the people caught in an ice storm survive.

A severe ice storm in 1998, in eastern Canada and upstate New York, USA, caused 4 million people to lose power, some for weeks.

An ice storm may sound wild and violent, but ice storms can actually be quite peaceful. However, they are still dangerous! They occur when very cold rain falls in freezing cold weather. The rain is liquid, but as soon as it lands on icy cold roads, houses, and trees, it freezes solid. Over time, a layer of very thick, heavy, slippery ice builds up. As well as causing skidding accidents on roads, ice can weigh down tree branches, roofs, and power lines until they snap.

WHAT TO DO

WHEN AN ICE STORM STRIKES:

If possible, stay indoors. Falling ice, tree branches, and power lines can be deadly. Driving in an ice storm is a bad idea, as roads are slippery and can be blocked by fallen trees.

IF YOU'RE CUT OFF:

Ice storms can cut off electricity and communications cables, leaving you isolated. Stay in and wait for the emergency services to check your home.

COMBAT THE COLD:

If you're cut off with no heating, try to keep warm. Everyone in the house should gather in one room with blankets, duvets, hats, and gloves. If you have a coal or wood fire, or stove with a proper flue or chimney, keep it lit and huddle around it.

TOP TIP! Never, ever bring a barbecue or other outdoor fire device indoors to keep you warm. They can give off poisonous fumes and have killed several people in past ice storms.

HAILSTORM

Hail is made up of hailstones – hard balls of ice that fall from the clouds. Hail forms inside thunderclouds. Each hailstone starts as a tiny object, such as a speck of dust, a small seed, or even a small insect. As strong winds blow it around inside the cloud, it bumps into icy cold raindrops. They freeze solid around it, building up layers of ice. When the hailstone is heavy enough, it falls. Ice is heavy, so even small hailstones can cause a lot of damage. And sometimes, giant hailstones fall in terrifying torrents.

WHAT TO DO

IF THERE'S A RISK OF HAIL:

It's hard to predict a hailstorm, but hail happens most often during thunderstorms. So if thunderstorms are in the forecast, avoid going out into remote areas or doing outdoor activities.

HUGE HAILSTONE

Hailstones can be as small as peas, or as big as golf balls. The biggest hailstone on record fell on Aurora, Nebraska, USA in 2003. It measured an incredible 18 cm (7 in) across.

DANGER RATING

RISK RATING: 💀 💀 💀 💀

Most parts of the world experience hail several times a year.

SURVIVAL RATING: 95%

Hail can be deadly, but generally only if the hailstones are unusually large.

DURING A HAILSTORM:

Stay indoors and keep away from windows, as the hail could break a window and shower you with glass. If you're out and about, and the hail is so heavy it seems dangerous, shelter under a doorway, a park bench, or even a parked car. If you're in a moving car, you should stop somewhere safe and huddle into the middle of the vehicle, away from the windows. Take care, as hail can make the ground slippery.

FROG FALL

Can it really rain frogs? The answer is yes, and it can also rain toads, fish, birds, jellyfish, and various other animals! These mysterious "falls" are very rare, but they have been reported around the world. Experts think that sometimes a waterspout — a kind of tornado over water — sucks up sea or lake animals and carries them over land, where they fall back down. Flocks of birds may fall like rain after flying into violent stormclouds.

DANGER RATING

RISK RATING: ☠
Showers of animals are pretty rare — and it's even less likely that one will fall on you.

SURVIVAL RATING: 95%
Animal falls have not claimed many lives, but a falling animal could be dangerous if it hits you.

WHAT TO DO

IF IT RAINS ANIMALS:
These events are very rare and cannot be predicted. If you suddenly find frogs, fish, or other animals falling around you, head for shelter immediately. The danger is that you will be so amazed or fascinated, you'll forget to run for cover! But even a small frog or fish falling from a great height could seriously injure you.

AFTER THE SHOWER:
When the weird weather has cleared, you might be tempted to go and examine the animals. Take care — animals have been known to survive the fall, and they may bite or sting.

DID YOU KNOW?
Animal showers have been happening for thousands of years. Frog and fish falls were reported in medieval times and in ancient Greece.

SANDSTORM

Sandstorms occur when a strong wind picks up a lot of sand and carries it through the air. The same thing can happen with dust during a drought.

Sandstorms and dust storms are dangerous because they fill the air with particles, making it hard to see and breathe. They can cause car and aeroplane accidents, and damage homes by dumping heavy sand on them.

DANGER RATING

RISK RATING: ☠ ☠ ☠
Sandstorms and dust storms are a common risk in dry areas.

SURVIVAL RATING: 90%
You're very likely to survive a sandstorm, especially if you have a car or building to shelter in.

WHAT TO DO

BE PREPARED:
If you're travelling in a dry area – especially if there are warnings of sandstorms – keep a lookout for them. Carry a safety kit, with eye goggles, a breathing mask, and a supply of drinking water.

IF YOU SEE A SANDSTORM COMING:
Run inside a building, and close all the doors and windows. If you're in a car, you might be able get away from the storm if it is a long way off. If it closes in, drive the car off the road. Close the windows and air vents, and turn off the lights (as they can make another car try to follow you). Stay put until the storm passes.

IF YOU'RE ON FOOT:
Protect your eyes with goggles or glasses, and put on a breathing mask or tie a wet cloth or scarf around your face. Avoid low ground, and shelter behind a rock. As the storm passes, curl up on the ground and cover your head with your arms.

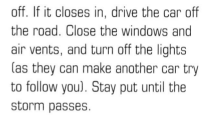

A haboob, a type of sandstorm featuring a fast-moving wall of sand and dust, moves in on a livestock market in Sudan.

DID YOU KNOW? Camels are used to sandstorms. They just close their eyes and nostrils. A camel can provide shelter if it sits down; you can curl up beside it.

SAND COLLAPSE

A sandy beach or dune might not look dangerous, but if sand falls on top of you, it can be very serious. If you don't get out fast, you can run out of air. Seaside and desert sand dunes can drop sand on people unexpectedly. They can also fall down if you try to dig into them to make a tunnel or cave. Even digging a big hole on the beach can be dangerous. If the hole is deep, the sides can suddenly cave in and cover you with sand.

WHAT TO DO

BE SAFE AROUND SAND:
Avoid sand dunes during storms and high winds, and watch out for safety signs and warnings in sand dune areas. Never dig under a sand dune. On the beach, don't dig big holes in the sand.

IF SAND FALLS ON YOU:
If you see it coming, try to jump out of the way. If sand is landing on you, curl into a ball and cup your hands over your face to make a breathing space. Try to stay calm and wait for help.

IF SAND FALLS ON SOMEONE ELSE:
You need to dig them out as fast as possible. Yell for help and get as many people as you can to dig with you. Meanwhile, ask someone to call an ambulance.

DANGER RATING

RISK RATING: ☠ ☠
There are sand accidents every year, but you can reduce the risk if you know how to prevent them.

SURVIVAL RATING: 30%
Being trapped under sand is very dangerous indeed – you need to get out fast to survive.

DANGER
THIS AREA IS LIABLE TO COLLAPSE FROM OLD MINEWORK

TOP TIP! It's OK to dig in sand to fill a bucket or make a sandcastle moat. But to be safe, make sure the holes are no deeper than knee high.

DUST DEVIL

A dust devil is a spinning spiral of wind that picks up dust or sand as it whirls along. It is similar to a tornado, except that dust devils usually form in hot, clear weather.

Dust devils are usually small — sometimes only as big as a person — and most are not harmful. But sometimes they can be much bigger — up to 10 metres (33 feet) wide and hundreds of metres high. The strong wind and flying particles in a dust devil can be dangerous.

DANGER RATING

RISK RATING: ☠ ☠ ☠
Dust devils are quite common in warm, dry areas.

SURVIVAL RATING: 95%
Dust devils have been known to harm people, but it's unlikely.

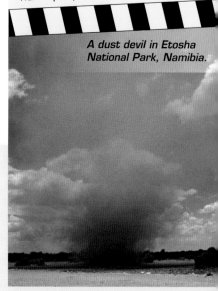

A dust devil in Etosha National Park, Namibia.

WHAT TO DO

DUST DEVIL CONDITIONS:
Dust devils are most likely to form in dry, flat places during hot, still weather. They happen when the sun heats up the ground, causing a column of hot air to rise upwards. So keep a lookout for them in hot, calm, dry, or desert areas.

IF YOU SEE A DUST DEVIL:
A dust devil looks like a tall spinning column or funnel of dust or sand. If you see one, you may be tempted to look more closely, but it's best to stay away — just in case. Shelter inside a building or vehicle, and watch from a safe distance.

IF YOU'RE CAUGHT IN A DUST DEVIL:
As in any sandstorm, crouch down and cover your face and head. If your car accidentally drives into a dust devil, slow down, and stop until it has passed by.

DID YOU KNOW?

Dust devils go by several different names. A dust devil can also be called a dancing devil, a dust whirl, or a willy-willy.

WATERSPOUT

Like a tornado or a dust devil, a waterspout is a towering, swirling wind spiral. The difference is that it happens over water, and sucks water up into it. Waterspouts can occur when a tornado forms over the ocean.

They usually form in cloudy weather because of the way warm, damp air moves over the water. They are found on lakes or on the sea, usually close to the shore. The main danger from waterspouts is that they can upturn boats or swamp them with water.

WHAT TO DO

IF YOU SEE A WATERSPOUT:

If you're in a boat, turn it around and sail away from the waterspout. If possible, go back to shore, as more waterspouts could form. Life rafts should be ready to launch. Stay in a cabin if possible, as a waterspout could upturn the boat or wash you overboard.

A huge waterspout off the northern Dutch coast above the Wadden Sea.

IF YOU'RE SWIMMING:

Swim away from the waterspout and get out of the water as soon as you can. If you are very close to a waterspout, try to stay calm. Tread water gently to save energy, and hold your breath if water swirls over you. Swim for the shore as soon as you can.

DANGER RATING

RISK RATING: 💀 💀 💀
Waterspouts are well known in tropical areas, and can happen around the world.

SURVIVAL RATING: 90%
A waterspout can easily sink a boat, but you should be able to get away from it first.

SEA MONSTERS

Long ago, sailors' reports of waterspouts may have given rise to legends about giant sea serpents attacking boats.

LIGHTNING

Lightning is one of the most spectacular events in nature. It's a giant electric spark, crackling between the clouds and the ground. It carries a huge amount of electrical energy — sometimes over 100 million volts — and can be as hot as 30,000°C, or 54,000°F – six times hotter than the surface of the Sun. And that means being struck by lightning can give someone a deadly electric shock.

WHAT TO DO

DON'T RISK A STRIKE:
Lightning happens during thunderstorms, and there will usually be a weather warning. Don't go out hiking, boating, or playing sports in a thunderstorm or if one is forecast.

DANGER RATING

RISK RATING: ☠ ☠
Thunderstorms and lightning are common, but being struck by lightning is pretty unlikely.

SURVIVAL RATING: 75%
About three quarters of people who are struck by lightning survive, though they may not always make a full recovery.

A lightning storm strikes downtown Los Angeles, USA.

DURING A THUNDERSTORM:
Stay indoors, and stay away from doors and windows, water, metal objects, and electrical appliances. Do not use phones or headphones – if lightning strikes the house, electricity could flow through them.

DID YOU KNOW?

Roy Sullivan, a park ranger from Virginia, USA, survived being struck by lightning seven times between 1942 and 1977.

IF YOU'RE STUCK OUTDOORS:
Avoid water, high ground, and open spaces, trees, and tents. Try to find shelter in a building or a car. Don't touch any metal. If there's no shelter, crouch down with your feet together and put your hands over your ears.

BALL LIGHTNING

Ball lightning is a very strange and little understood phenomenon. It usually appears as a glowing, floating ball, around 15 to 30 centimetres (6–12 inches) across. It may float around for up to a minute, before disappearing with a popping sound or a small explosion.

Ball lightning can happen during thunderstorms, but has been recorded in normal weather, too. It has been seen from buildings, boats, submarines, and aircraft. Scientists think it has something to do with electricity, but they don't know exactly what it is.

DANGER RATING

RISK RATING: ☠ ☠

Ball lightning is fairly rare, and very hard to predict.

SURVIVAL RATING: 95%

Most ball lightning does not harm people, but it can can cause burns and make holes in solid objects.

WHAT TO DO

IF YOU SEE BALL LIGHTNING:

Stay calm, and move away from the lightning slowly and carefully. Don't panic and run away wildly or run backwards – you could trip and get hurt.

There's not much point shutting yourself away in another room, as ball lightning can move through solid doors and walls. Instead, watch the lightning to make sure it doesn't get too close to you. It will most likely float away and disappear after a few seconds.

One of the very few existing photographs of ball lightning.

LAB LIGHTNING

Scientists are trying to create ball lightning artificially, by running electrical energy through various substances. They have succeeded in making several small glowing balls.

Temperatures reached a blistering 41.1°C (106°F) in New Jersey in 200

HEAT WAVE

A heat wave is a period of unusually hot summer weather, 10 degrees or more above average. A combination of sunshine, lack of wind, and high humidity (moisture in the air) drives the temperature up.

Heat waves are often worse in cities. In the countryside, plants and trees have a cooling effect and the temperature falls at night. But in cities, buildings and roads store heat all night long. Hot weather might not sound dangerous, but heat waves can actually cause thousands of deaths.

DANGER RATING

RISK RATING: ☠ ☠ ☠
Heat waves are a danger every summer, and some experts think they are getting worse.

SURVIVAL RATING: 90%
Of the people affected by a heat wave, most will survive.
But if heat waves affect whole countries, they can claim many lives.

WHAT TO DO

IF A HEAT WAVE IS PREDICTED:
Don't plan any strenuous activities, such as hiking, sports, or building projects. Stock up on sunscreen and make sure you have a sunhat. Keep emergency numbers handy.

DURING A HEAT WAVE:
Stay indoors in the middle of the day. Use air-conditioning if you have it, or if not, close curtains, open windows, and use fans to keep your house cool. Drink lots of water and cold drinks – but avoid coffee, strong tea, and alcohol, as they can make your body lose water. Outdoors, wear a hat and long, light, loose clothing. Slow down, and avoid running around.

IF SOMEONE GETS TOO HOT People can die during heat waves from overheating – especially the old, young, or unwell. The signs include feeling hot, sick, and dizzy, a red rash and no sweating. If this happens, call an ambulance. Use cold water to cool them down.

DROUGHT

A drought is an unusually dry period, often caused by low rainfall. Droughts can have other causes, too, such as people using up too much water for watering crops.

In most countries, droughts last for a few weeks or months, but the rain eventually returns. Very severe droughts, however, can cause disaster, especially in developing countries, where people may be very poor and have nowhere else to move to. A long-term drought can destroy crops and lead to a deadly famine (food shortage) as well as dangerous water shortages.

DANGER RATING

RISK RATING: ☠ ☠ ☠
Droughts are a normal part of weather patterns.

SURVIVAL RATING: 90%
It's unlikely you'll experience a really dangerous drought.

In drought areas, like here in Mali, water supplies are used over and over, allowing diseases to spread.

WHAT TO DO

IF A DROUGHT IS PREDICTED:
Try to reduce the amount of water you use. Don't leave taps running, have quick showers or shallow baths, and avoid watering your lawn or garden.

DURING A DROUGHT:
You still need to save water, but make sure you drink enough. The weather will be dry and probably hot, making you sweat, so you need to drink a lot. If water is really short, save it all for drinking – don't waste it on washing. Listen for official instructions in case you are told to leave the area. Droughts can also lead to other problems such as wildfires and dust storms, so be on your guard.

TOP TIP! One good way to save water is to catch rainwater in a bucket. The water can then be used for watering plants.

LOST IN THE DESERT

Deserts are very dry areas where few things can survive. Some are almost all bare rock or sand; others may have small bushes or cacti growing in them. Most deserts are hot during the day, but get cold at night. In some countries, such as the USA and Australia, a lot of roads run through deserts – drivers can lose their way and cars can break down.

WHAT TO DO

DESERT SAFETY:

If you're going to travel in a desert area, make sure you take some spare fuel, high-energy foods, blankets, a map, sun hats and sunglasses, and lots of water.

IF YOU GET LOST:

If you're in a car that breaks down, stay with the car. It will be too hot inside, so sit beside it in the shade. Sit on a box or stool, not on the ground, as the ground will be much hotter than the air. Keep covered up with long, loose clothing and a hat. At night, snuggle up inside the car, wrapped in blankets. Drink as much water as you need.

DANGER RATING

RISK RATING: ☠ ☠
Most journeys are uneventful, but deserts are dangerous.

SURVIVAL RATING: 60%
Humans can only survive 3 or 4 days without water – if you run out, you're in serious danger. If people know you're missing, you should be found in time.

If you're lost on foot, look for trees, rocks, or cliffs that could provide shade.

SIGNAL FOR HELP:

If you have a mobile phone, use it to call for help. Arrange branches or stones in a large triangle shape (an international SOS signal), or simply spell SOS. Use a mirror or any shiny object to reflect the sun to signal to passing aircraft.

LOST AT THE POLES

Explorers battle through the ice and snow on their way to the South Pole.

The poles are the extreme northern and southern points of Earth, farthest away from the equator. The regions around the poles are freezing cold, and often covered with ice and snow and scoured by howling winds. Few people go there at all, but you could get lost there if a vehicle breaks down during an expedition, or if you're in a plane that crashes.

WHAT TO DO

IF YOU CRASH OR BREAK DOWN:

Try to phone or radio for help. Create an SOS signal using whatever you can — bags, boxes, or vehicle parts. Everyone should stay together and stay with the vehicle, using it as shelter. Don't wander off — you could fall down a crevasse or into icy water, or get buried in snow. Keep your body covered up, and huddle together with other people. If you have any fuel, make a fire and melt snow to make drinking water. Avoid melting ice or snow in your mouth — it will make you even colder.

DANGER RATING

RISK RATING: ☠
Few people go to the poles except on well-organized, official trips, so getting lost is rare.

SURVIVAL RATING: 20%
It's so cold at the poles that surviving when lost is tough.

HOW COLD? The average temperature in the Arctic (the area around the North Pole) is about -22°C (-8°F). In the Antarctic, around the South Pole, it's even colder at around -50°C (-58°F).

LOST ON A MOUNTAIN

Lots of people go hiking, climbing, rafting, and skiing in mountain areas, and have lots of fun. But mountains can be scary and dangerous, too. They have steep slopes and cliffs, strong winds, and sometimes snow and ice. People often get lost, separated from their group, or stuck because of an injury such as a twisted ankle.

DANGER RATING

RISK RATING: ☠ ☠ ☠
A lot of people visit mountains, and people get lost or injured quite often.

SURVIVAL RATING: 70%
It depends on the mountain. On some, getting lost is disastrous – but on most, you'll probably be rescued.

WHAT TO DO

MOUNTAIN SAFETY:

Be prepared before you go up into the mountains. Wear hiking boots and outdoor clothes, and take drinks, snacks, a whistle, and a warm, windproof coat. Plan your route, and tell someone where you will be and when you'll be back. Check the forecast – don't set out if it's bad.

IF YOU'RE LOST:

Your map might help you, or the view may show you a safe route down the mountain. If it's daylight and good weather, you can probably walk to safety. Follow valleys and streams downhill.

Retreating down an icy cliff in a blizzard is extremely difficult and dangerous.

IF YOU GET STUCK:

Bad weather, nightfall, or an injury can trap you on a mountain. Look for a place to shelter, such as between rocks, and call for help on a mobile phone if possible. If not, blow your whistle (or make a whistling noise) three times, wait a minute then blow it again. Huddle up and wait for rescue.

TOP TIP! If you see a rescue helicopter, you can signal to it that you need help by sticking your arms up and out in a big 'Y' shape.

FALLEN INTO A VOLCANIC CRATER

A volcano's crater is the bowl-shaped hollow at the top, where lava and rocks burst out during an eruption. Craters are usually round with steep sides and a flat bottom. Some active volcanoes are considered safe for tourists to visit, so there are trails leading up to the edge of the crater – and sometimes, people fall in.

WHAT TO DO

NO CRATER CRAZINESS!

Volcanoes are so exciting that tourists sometimes climb over safety barriers, or clamber down inside the edge of a crater, to get a better look and take photos. Never, ever do this! The steep slopes and loose rocks mean you can slip easily.

DID YOU KNOW?

Volcanoes can be "dormant" – which means "sleeping" – for many years, then suddenly become active and start erupting again.

IF YOU FALL IN:

Drop anything you're holding and use your arms and legs to try to steady yourself. When you come to a stop, keep still and wave and call to people on the edge of the crater to get help. Don't get up and try to climb back out by yourself – you could fall again. Some craters contain dangerous hot lava, hot water, or steam jets that could seriously injure you. Stay calm and wait to be rescued.

The crater of an active volcano in Ethiopia.

DANGER RATING

RISK RATING: ☠ ☠

Volcano craters are not safe places to be, but most people avoid danger by acting sensibly.

SURVIVAL RATING: 50%

If you do fall into a crater, you'll probably need a lot of luck and help to get out safely.

SWEPT AWAY IN A RIVER

Rivers are often far more dangerous than they look. There may be strong currents and overhanging ledges under the surface. Water that doesn't seem to be flowing very fast can still carry you away quickly. And if there are rocks in the river, you could be thrown against them. It's important to take care near dangerous rivers and avoid being swept away in the first place.

DANGER RATING

RISK RATING: ☠ ☠ ☠
Even rivers that look calm and safe can sweep people away.

SURVIVAL RATING: 40%
Being swept away by a river is extremely dangerous.

Fast-flowing rivers like this, the Brathay in England's Lake District, are especially dangerous.

WHAT TO DO

RIVER SAFETY:

Near rivers, stay away from the bank – don't lean over to try to peer in, touch the water, or grab something you've dropped. Watch out for wet, slippery rocks and muddy banks. Don't try to wade across a river instead of using a bridge. And don't swim or paddle in rivers, except at well-known safe swimming places, with sensible adults or with an organized group.

IF YOU ARE SWEPT AWAY:

Don't try to struggle against the current – you'll wear yourself out. Instead, stay calm, and swim sideways, aiming for the nearest bank, as you are swept along. Try to steer around rocks. If you can, climb out of the river and move away from the edge. Otherwise, grab on to a branch or rock on the bank. Shout for help, hang on tight, and wait to be rescued.

WATER POWER Rushing water just 30 cm (12 in) deep is enough to sweep you off your feet and carry you away.

SWEPT OVER A WATERFALL

People are swept over waterfalls every year – few survive. Waterfalls occur where a river plunges over a ledge of hard rock. Often the falling water has worn away a deep pool at the base. Even if the fall is not high, it can be hard to escape from the churning pool.

WHAT TO DO

DON'T LET IT HAPPEN:
Never swim, play, or paddle in water upstream from a waterfall. Avoid standing on the bank or rocks near the top of a waterfall, close to the water's edge.

IF YOU ARE SWEPT AWAY:
Try to get out of the water at once, or grab a rock, branch, or tree root and hold on until you are rescued. If you are swept over the waterfall, cover your head and hold your breath. After you land, kick upwards to try to reach the surface, and let the river carry you away from the waterfall. Swim for the bank once you are in calmer water.

DANGER RATING

RISK RATING: ☠ ☠
Even if you do fall into a river, you probably won't be near a waterfall.

SURVIVAL RATING: 20%
People have survived going over waterfalls, but they are the minority.

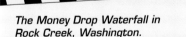

The Money Drop Waterfall in Rock Creek, Washington.

DID YOU KNOW?

In 1960, a 7-year-old boy named Roger Woodward miraculously survived being swept over one of the world's most powerful waterfalls, Niagara Falls. He was wearing a life vest and was rescued from the plunge pool by a tour boat.

LOST AT SEA IN A BOAT OR RAFT

You could end up adrift at sea for several reasons. You could be in a small motorboat that breaks down, or you could run out of fuel and lose your way. Or you could be on a bigger boat or ship that sinks, leaving you in a lifeboat or life raft. The dangers you face include cold and wind, sunburn, and water shortages.

WHAT TO DO

KEEP WARM:
Wrap up in all the clothes you have, including wet suits and diving suits. Shelter from the wind.

AVOID THE SUN:
If there is strong sunshine, you could get bad sunburn or sunstroke. Shade yourself with a hat, sheet, or tarpaulin.

COLLECT WATER:
Water is more important than food – only eat if you have water to drink, too, as digesting food uses up water in your body. Drink the fresh water you have when you need to. Use any containers you have to collect rainwater, and store it carefully. If you find chunks

DANGER RATING

RISK RATING: ☠ ☠ ☠
People get lost at sea quite often, though they are usually rescued.

SURVIVAL RATING: 75%
In most cases, someone will be looking for you, and you have a good chance of survival.

of ice in the sea, you can melt them and drink them, as they should not be salty. Do not drink seawater, unless your raft has equipment for making it safe.

GET HELP:
If you see a ship or aircraft, send a signal with distress flares, a mirror to reflect the sunlight, or a torch at night. If you see land, paddle towards it with your hands or bits of wood.

TOP TIP! Before collecting rain in a container or plastic sheet, rinse the container in the sea. Otherwise, the buildup of salt on it from the sea spray will make your water salty.

ADRIFT AT SEA WITH NO BOAT

What if your boat sinks and you're left on your own in the open ocean? This situation is, of course, incredibly hazardous. But there's a lot you can do to make it safer. The most important thing to do is stay calm and save as much energy as you can.

DANGER RATING

RISK RATING: ☠ ☠
It's very unlikely this will happen, as most boats have life rafts.

SURVIVAL RATING: 30%
People do survive this situation, though they may have to wait in the sea for a long time.

WHAT TO DO

IF YOUR BOAT IS SINKING:

Try to grab something that will help you stay afloat, such as a life jacket or pieces of wooden wreckage. Once you are in the water, move away from the boat, as it can suck you downwards when it sinks.

IS IT A SHARK?

Don't worry if you feel something touching you in the water – it's probably NOT a shark. Shark attacks are actually quite rare. It's probably a smaller fish or even a friendly dolphin. Dolphins have been known to surround and support people stranded in the water.

STAY AFLOAT:

If you don't have a float, you may be able to make one by inflating a pair of trousers or a top. Tie up the arm or leg openings and blow air into the waist, then hold it closed. You may need to keep refilling it. Meanwhile, tread water slowly and calmly – don't panic. Save your energy for keeping you warm, and for shouting and waving if you see a boat.

Keep looking out for other floating objects that you can use.

CAUGHT IN A WHIRLPOOL

Moskstraumen in Norway is one of the world's most powerful whirlpools.

A whirlpool is a spiralling body of water in a sea, lake, or river. It can also be called a maelstrom or vortex, especially if the water is sucked downwards as well as going round and round.

Whirlpools usually form where fast-moving tides, or one river flowing into another, cause the water to flow in a huge spiral.

WHAT TO DO

IF YOU SEE A WHIRLPOOL:

If you see water moving in a swirling, churning pattern, stay away! Don't swim in the water, even in a different part of the river or bay. Boats should not go near the whirlpool – even large boats.

IF YOUR BOAT IS SUCKED IN:

The boat may lean to one side and spin around before starting to capsize. People have survived whirlpools by jumping off the boat and swimming to shore. It's usually safer to stay with the boat – stay up on deck in case it sinks.

IF YOU'RE IN A WHIRLPOOL WITH NO BOAT:

Tread water and look out for floating objects to hold on to. Paddle away from the middle of the whirlpool and call for help.

MYTHICAL MAELSTROM

In the Greek myth *The Odyssey*, the hero Odysseus must sail between Charybdis, a sea monster who creates whirlpools, and Scylla, a many-headed monster, to make his way home.

DANGER RATING

RISK RATING: ☠
Dangerous whirlpools are extremely rare.

SURVIVAL RATING: 60%
If you do end up in a whirlpool, things could get nasty, but you do have a reasonable chance of escape.

WASHED ASHORE ON A REMOTE ISLAND

If you fall off a boat or get shipwrecked, seeing an island where you can swim ashore is good news!

WHAT TO DO

MAKE IT ASHORE:

Aim for a gently sloping, sandy beach in a small bay, if possible. Swim towards the flattest part of the beach – this will make it easier to walk ashore. Try to stay in the trough between two waves. If a wave is about to break over you, turn to face it, dive under it, and come up in the trough behind it, then aim for the shore again. Once ashore, move far up the beach and make sure the tide can't cut you off.

FIND WATER AND FOOD:

You may find fresh water in a stream flowing into the sea, in pools among sand dunes, or trickling over rocks or cliffs behind the beach. Don't drink seawater – it will make you ill.

DANGER RATING

RISK RATING: ☠ ☠
This situation may happen a lot in films or cartoons, but it's very unusual in real life!

SURVIVAL RATING: 70%
If you're lucky enough to make it to dry land, you should survive.

Rock pools may contain fish, crabs, limpets, and abalone. Tropical islands may also have coconut and avocado trees.

FIND SHELTER:

Look for a cave (check it doesn't get cut off by the tide), or make a shelter by leaning branches and large leaves against a rock or tree.

EXPLORE THE ISLAND:

Walk around the island to look for food sources and campsites. Even uninhabited islands may have shelters left by previous visitors.

Only eat shellfish that are alive. You can tell they're alive if their shells are very hard to open.

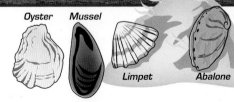

Oyster Mussel Limpet Abalone

LOST IN A CAVE

In many parts of the world, there are vast networks of cave passageways and chambers deep underground. Scientists studying wildlife and rocks, and cavers or spelunkers (people who go into caves for sport) explore them, and tourists can also go on cave tours. It's possible that you could get lost on a tour, or cut off by water or a rockfall.

DANGER RATING

RISK RATING: ☠ ☠
Most cave expeditions are led by experienced guides, so you're unlikely to get lost.

SURVIVAL RATING: 60%
Rescuers will be out looking for you, and should find you if you stay put.

WHAT TO DO

STAY TOGETHER, STAY WARM, AND STAY STILL:
Caves are full of dangers – cliffs, sharp rocks, and underground rivers and pools. And they are usually very, very dark. If you don't know your way, it's safer to stay still and wait to be found. If you are in a group, everyone should huddle together for warmth. Put on all the spare clothes, gloves, and hats you have to keep as warm as you can. Stay away from cave water, as getting wet will make you colder.

MAKE CONTACT:
If you have a mobile phone, use it to call for help. If it doesn't work, try again later. If you hear rescuers coming, call to them and shine torches to help them find you.

SAVE BATTERIES:
Stuck in the blackness of a deep cave, you'll probably want to switch on your torch. But it's better to keep it switched off and save the batteries for emergencies or for signalling to rescuers. The same goes for your mobile phone – switch it off when it's not in use, to save the batteries.

TOP TIP! If your torch runs out of batteries or you don't have one, a mobile phone can be used to shine a small amount of light.

STUCK ON A CLIFF FACE

Cliffs are very dangerous places. People can get hurt by falling off them, or by trying to climb up them without proper safety equipment. Even experienced climbers with ropes sometimes get stuck and have to be rescued. Rescuers sometimes climb the cliff using ropes to help the trapped person down, or they can use a rescue helicopter to airlift them to safety.

WHAT TO DO

CLIFF SENSE:
Be very, very careful near cliffs. Don't go near cliff edges, and never try to climb a cliff without proper ropes and an expert guide – unless you're escaping from another emergency, such as a shipwreck!

IF YOU GET STUCK:
You could get stuck on a cliff by falling down from the top, or by climbing up from the bottom. Wherever you are, try to lean in towards the cliff face, staying back from the edge of the rock or ledge you are on. Keep still, and breathe steadily. If you need to wave or shout for help, do so calmly and slowly.

STEEP SLOPES

You might think of a cliff as a vertical drop, but many cliffs are more like very steep slopes. If you fall down, you may be able to slide to a halt or stop on a ledge.

A rescuer dangles from a helicopter to save a boy from a cliff ledge.

DANGER RATING

RISK RATING: ☠ ☠ ☠
All cliffs are dangerous, especially when people aren't careful enough.

SURVIVAL RATING: 80%
If you're stuck on a cliff face, rescue will probably be coming soon.

IF YOU ARE INJURED:
Try to stop any bleeding by pressing your hand onto the wound. Keep any suspected broken bones as still as you can.

OUT ON THIN ICE

If possible, you should avoid walking over ice at all if you don't have to. But even if you try to avoid it, you could still end up on the ice after a fall or traffic accident. Ice more than 10 centimetres (4 inches) thick can support a person's weight. But even if the ice you are on feels safe, there could be thinner areas, especially on frozen rivers, and you could fall through.

DANGER RATING

RISK RATING: ☠ ☠ ☠ ☠

In many places, water freezes over every winter and it's easy to get into trouble.

SURVIVAL RATING: 90%

If you get off the ice quickly, you should be safe.

WHAT TO DO

DON'T RISK IT:

Don't be tempted to step out onto a frozen lake or river to see what happens. And don't decide to go onto the ice for just a second to retrieve a ball or bag – it can still break. People do activities such as ice fishing on very thick ice, but this is only safe when the ice has been carefully tested.

IF YOU ARE ON THIN ICE:

Lie down and spread out your arms and legs to spread your weight. Slither or roll towards the edge of the ice. Avoid ice that is cracked and aim for thicker ice – it looks clearer and bluer than thin ice. If you are on a section of ice surrounded by breaking ice, don't move. Lie still and shout for help.

DOG DISASTERS People sometimes risk their lives going onto thin ice to catch their runaway dog. Never do this! Remember you are probably heavier than your dog. On top of that, dogs can often scramble to safety themselves, even if they have fallen through the ice.

FALLEN THROUGH ICE

Falling through ice is very dangerous as the water underneath is icy cold. People can only survive in freezing cold water for a few minutes before they get too cold and numb to move. It's also possible to fall through a hole in the ice, then get trapped under the solid ice nearby and drown. It's vital to get out as soon as you can.

WHAT TO DO

AS YOU FALL:

If you feel yourself falling, lean back to help keep your head above water. The cold water will shock you and make you gasp, but stay as calm as you can and tread water.

TRY TO GET OUT:

Turn to face the direction you came from, as this is probably the strongest ice. Put your arms on the ice, lean forward and kick your legs behind you to try to "swim" out of the hole. You may need to rest halfway, with your upper body on the ice and your legs still in the water. Push against the other side of the hole. If the ice breaks, move forward and try again.

IF SOMEONE ELSE FALLS IN:

People often die going onto the ice to save someone else who has fallen through. Instead, rescuers should throw a rope, or scarves tied together, and pull the person out. If there's no rope, a long pole or plank may help the person to pull him or herself out. If going onto the ice is essential, the rescuer should tie a rope around his or her waist, with the other end tied to something on shore, and crawl, not walk, across the ice.

TOP TIP! You may be able to stick keys, jewellery, or a penknife into the ice to help pull yourself out.

DANGER RATING

RISK RATING: ☠ ☠ ☠
You should be able to avoid falling through ice, but sadly it happens to hundreds of people each year.

SURVIVAL RATING: 30%
It's difficult to survive unless you can get out of the water fast.

SINKING IN QUICKSAND

This young elephant waded into the waterhole to get a drink, but got stuck in the quicksand.

DANGER RATING

RISK RATING: ☠ ☠
Dangerous quicksand is rare.

SURVIVAL RATING: 90%
It's fairly easy to escape from quicksand, as long as you know what to do.

In adventure films, quicksand can suck people under in seconds. In real life, it's not really all that bad. Quicksand can form anywhere where sand, or sandy, silty mud, gets saturated with water. This can create a loose, semiliquid substance that you can sink into. However, you can float in quicksand, just as you can in water, so you're unlikely to go under.

WHAT TO DO

AVOID QUICKSAND:

Look out for quicksand when walking on beaches and other sandy areas. It's hard to see from a distance, but when you step on it, it may wobble and ripple like jelly – if it does, step back. You can also use a long pole to test for quicksand.

TOP TIP! The more quicksand vibrates and shakes about, the more liquid it gets. When you are sinking, panicking and thrashing around may make you sink faster. But when you are pulling your legs out, it may help to shake and wiggle them.

IF YOU GET STUCK IN QUICKSAND:

If you walk over quicksand, you may start to sink downwards. Drop any heavy bags you are carrying and if possible, try to kick off your shoes. Lean over and lie down on your back – try to do this before you sink any deeper than waist height! While "floating" on your back, you can slowly drag your legs and feet back up to the surface. Once you're out, roll or wriggle away over the surface of the quicksand to safety.

It's hard to spot quicksand just by looking at it – it often looks like normal sand.

STUCK IN A SWAMP

A swamp is a wet, soggy area with a combination of mud, water, and marshy ground. There are usually trees, grasses, and water plants. It can be very hard to find your way through a swamp, as you can't see far and you can easily wander into waist-deep water. Worst of all, you can sink into sticky mud and get trapped.

WHAT TO DO

SWAMP SAFETY:

It's a good idea to avoid swamps, unless you're with an organized group or a knowledgeable guide. But if you are in one, the best way to stay safe is to step on tufts of grass and bunches of water reeds. If you can find a long stick, use it to test the ground before you step on it. Avoid pools and flat, muddy areas where you could sink.

IF YOU GET STUCK:

If you feel yourself sinking into mud, lie down quickly so that you float, and swim or roll to firmer ground. If you react too slowly and your feet get stuck, you might be able to pull yourself out by grabbing a tree branch.

IF YOU'RE LOST:

If other people know where you are and will come looking for you, find a safe place to wait. If you can do so safely, climb a tree. It will keep you away from swamp animals such as crocodiles, and it will make it easier to wave to rescue helicopters.

DANGER RATING

RISK RATING: ☠ ☠
Swamps are hard to travel in, so it's unlikely you'll get lost in one.

SURVIVAL RATING: 60%
Escaping from a swamp could be difficult, especially if it's full of crocodiles.

SWAMP SURVIVOR

In 2007, an Australian farmer was stranded in a crocodile-infested swamp after his horse carried him the wrong way. He was found by a search helicopter after spending seven nights in a tree!

CUT OFF BY THE TIDE

Tides exist at the coast because of the gravity of the moon. It pulls at the sea, making it rise up the beach and then fall back down twice a day. Sometimes, you can reach a sheltered bay, island, or sea cave at low tide by walking along the beach, but when high tide comes, the route is cut off by the rising water. You may become trapped between the rising tide and high cliffs.

WHAT TO DO

WATCH THE TIDES:

At the beach, always keep an eye on where you are and how close the tide is. Move away from areas that could be cut off while the tide is still out. You can often check in advance when the tide will come in, at bulletin boards on the beach. Tide timetables are sometimes posted on the Internet, too.

IF YOU ARE CUT OFF:

Call for help as soon as you can. If you have a phone, call the emergency services and ask for the coast guard, who may rescue you by boat or helicopter. You can also try to get help by shouting to anyone you can see on the land or in a boat.

DANGER RATING

RISK RATING: ☠ ☠ ☠ ☠
People get cut off by the tide all the time. It can happen very quickly with little warning.

SURVIVAL RATING: 90%
If you raise the alarm fast, you'll probably be rescued.

Twenty-one Chinese migrant workers died in Morecambe Bay, England, in 2005 when they were caught by fast-rising tides as they searched for cockles, a shellfish delicacy.

TOP TIP! Avoid playing or exploring in caves on the beach. The tide could come in while you are inside and can't see it coming.

CAUGHT IN A RIPTIDE

A riptide is not a tide, but a strong current of water flowing from the beach out into the sea. It can also be called a rip current, or a rip. A riptide forms when water brought ashore by breaking waves gathers and flows back into the sea along a narrow channel. Riptides can sweep swimmers out to sea, but only a short distance.

Surfers use riptides to get a lift out to deeper water.

WHAT TO DO

AVOID RIPTIDES:

You can sometimes spot a riptide. The water in the current may look calmer, flatter, and darker than the surrounding waves. You should also avoid swimming at low tide, when riptides are more common. And don't swim close to piers and jetties, as riptides often form there.

IF YOU'RE CAUGHT IN THE CURRENT:

When you feel the water sweeping you away, don't panic. People usually only drown in riptides if they struggle and try to swim against the current.

Instead, tread water calmly until the current stops, then swim back to the shore. Or, if you're a good swimmer, you can try swimming sideways, along the beach, to escape from the current.

DANGER RATING

RISK RATING: ☠ ☠ ☠ ☠

Riptides are very common and thousands and thousands of people are caught in them every year.

SURVIVAL RATING: 90%

You should be able to survive a riptide if you know what to do.

RIPPING ALONG

The water in a riptide can flow at a speed of up to 10 kph (6 mph). This is quite a slow speed if you're running, but it's much faster than you can swim.

LOST ON A GLACIER

A glacier is a massive, slow-moving river of ice. Glaciers form in cold places, such as high mountains, where heavy snowfall packs down into solid ice over time. Mountaineers often have to cross glaciers when they climb high mountains, and skiers often ski over snow-covered glaciers, too. As well as being cold, glaciers are dangerous because of the deep cracks, or crevasses, that form in them.

DANGER RATING

RISK RATING:
Glacier climbing is usually done in organized groups, so you shouldn't get lost.

SURVIVAL RATING: 60%
If you do get well and truly lost on a glacier, you'll need skill and luck to reach safety.

WHAT TO DO

GLACIER SAFETY:
You should only venture onto a glacier in a properly led group with an experienced guide, carrying climbing ropes and equipment. Always follow the leader's instructions and stay roped together with everyone else.

IF YOU GET LOST:
You still could end up on a glacier after getting lost on a mountain, or after a plane crash. If the glacier is snowy, snow could cover the crevasses and make them invisible, so it's best to stay still. Call for help, and wrap up warm in all the clothing you have with you. If there's no snow and you can see the crevasses clearly, you can move away from them and aim sideways to get off the glacier. If you are skiing and get lost on a glacier, keep your skis on, as they spread your weight over a bigger area and make you less likely to fall down a crevasse.

TOP TIP! You should always wear crampons when walking on a glacier. These are special spikes that fit on to your boots to help your feet grip the ice.

FALLEN DOWN A CREVASSE

Crevasses are scary and very dangerous. Some are just a few feet deep, but others are much deeper – as deep as the glacier itself, which can be over 100 metres (330 feet) thick. Falling down a crevasse can be deadly. If you survive the fall, you could be injured and will probably have to depend on other climbers to get you out.

WHAT TO DO

BE PREPARED:
Sensible climbers always cross crevasses in groups, roped together so that if one person falls down a crevasse, the others can pull him or her out. You should always wear a climbing helmet, as many people who fall down crevasses get head injuries.

IF YOU FALL:
If you're on a rope, you may be able to climb out or be pulled out by the other climbers. If you're not, you'll fall to the bottom of the crevasse. Try to stay in a safe place, away from any deeper cracks you can see. Wrap up well and curl up in a ball to keep warm while you wait for rescue. Call to people on the surface to let them know where you are.

If you're alone, your only hope is to move along the bottom of the crevasse to see if you can find a way out. Some crevasses slope back up to the surface, or lead out of a hole in the side of the glacier.

DANGER RATING

RISK RATING: ☠ ☠
Though falling down a crevasse isn't very common, crevasses do claim lives every year.

SURVIVAL RATING: 50%
Falling down a cevasse is serious, but having climbing ropes will improve your chances.

MIRACLE ESCAPE In 1985, a climber named Joe Simpson fell down a crevasse in Peru. Though he had a broken leg, he managed to crawl out of the crevasse and down the glacier to safety.

LOST IN THE JUNGLE

The word "jungle" is usually used to mean a rainforest – a type of thick, humid, rainy forest found in the tropical regions of the world. Rainforests can be dangerous as they are home to lots of biting bugs and large wild animals.

WHAT TO DO

TRAVEL SAFELY:

You should not try to walk through a tropical jungle except along a clear tourist trail, or with an experienced guide. However, if you do go into the jungle, be prepared. Wear strong boots and take clothing with full-length arms and legs, snacks, a water bottle, a raincoat, a penknife, and matches.

IF YOU GET LOST:

First, shout and wave to help your travel companions find you again. If that doesn't work, you'll have to wait to be rescued. Stay in one place and wear lots of clothes to protect against biting insects. If it rains, put your coat on and try to avoid getting soaked. If you have anything brightly coloured or shiny, hang it on a branch to help rescuers spot you.

DANGER RATING

RISK RATING: ☠ ☠
You're unlikely to be wandering through a rainforest without a guide.

SURVIVAL RATING: 60%
It is very hard to find people in the jungle, so getting lost is NOT a good idea!

FOOD AND WATER:

Drink your own water supply first. If you need more, take water from a fast-flowing stream or spring, or collect rain in your raincoat. If you go near a stream or river, take care and watch out for crocodiles or alligators and dangerous fish. You may find fruit such as bananas, mangoes, and avocados, but only eat them if you are 100 per cent sure you know what they are.

DID YOU KNOW?

In 2007, two French hikers were lost in the rainforest in French Guiana, South America, for almost two months! They survived by eating turtles and spiders.

TRAPPED BY A FALLEN TREE

A big, tall tree toppling over can be a deadly danger. A tree trunk, or even a large branch, can be so heavy that if it pins you to the ground, you'll never be able to escape on your own.

In forests, parks, and even backyards, trees can fall down when they grow old and die, or they can be blown down by heavy winds. Sometimes people get trapped when a tree they are cutting down falls on them.

DANGER RATING

RISK RATING: ☠ ☠ ☠
Falling trees kill hundreds of people every year.

SURVIVAL RATING: 75%
Being trapped by a fallen tree is dangerous and scary, but you should be rescued.

TOP TIP! No one should ever try to cut down a tree if they don't know exactly what they are doing. If a tree needs to come down, call a trained tree feller.

WHAT TO DO

IF A TREE IS FALLING:
You may be warned that a tree is about to fall by a loud creaking sound. You'll have a few seconds before it hits the ground. Stay calm, look for the tree, and figure out which way it is falling. Run out of reach or get on the other side of the tree, whichever is quickest.

IF THE TREE LANDS ON YOU:
Try to move your head and body out of the way of the tree and cover your head with your arms. If part of your body gets pinned under the tree, you may want to try to pull free, but if you're stuck fast, stop trying, as this will wear you out. Instead, stay calm and shout to passers-by, or use a phone to call for help. While you wait, stay calm, and keep warm by putting on any extra clothes you have with you.

BOA CONSTRICTOR

Boas and pythons are constrictor snakes. This means that instead of giving their prey a poisonous bite, they wrap their bodies around their victims and squeeze them. As they squeeze more and more tightly, the victim cannot breathe and gets suffocated or strangled. The snake then opens its mouth wide and swallows its prey whole. Even a snake that is too small to eat a human could try to constrict and strangle someone. Constrictors are found around the world, mainly in tropical areas.

WHAT TO DO

TAKE CARE WITH SNAKES:
If you see a snake in the wild, you should avoid it. However, many people keep boas and pythons as pets, and you need to be careful with them, too. Never let a pet constrictor snake, especially a large one, coil around your body or neck.

IF A CONSTRICTOR ATTACKS:
If a constrictor wraps itself around you, stay calm, take a deep breath and hold it in. The snake will take its chance to squeeze when you breathe out. Try to control the snake's head and unwrap its body from around you.

Get someone to help you if possible. As soon as you are free, run away from the snake or lock it in its tank or in another room.

DANGER RATING

RISK RATING: ☠ ☠
Being squeezed and swallowed by a snake is very rare, but it does happen.

SURVIVAL RATING: 60%
Most snakes are not big enough to swallow you. With help, you may be able to get away.

DID YOU KNOW?

Large constrictor snakes, such as the African rock python and the reticulated python, can grow up to 8 to 10 m (26–33 ft) long.

They have been known to kill and swallow whole bears and antelopes, as well as humans.

RATTLESNAKE BITE

There are about 50 different types of rattlesnakes. They live in North, Central, and South America, especially in hot, dry areas. These very poisonous snakes get their name because they have a "rattle" on their tails, made of rings of hard, dried, dead skin. The snake can shake its rattle as a warning when it feels threatened. That's good news, because it helps you avoid rattlesnakes and stay safe. If you are bitten, you must get help fast.

WHAT TO DO

SNAKE SENSE:

If you're going to be in rattlesnake country, wear tough boots and long trousers. Watch out for snakes, and don't stick your hands into bushes or holes without checking for snakes first.

KEEP YOUR DISTANCE:

If you see or hear a rattlesnake, move away from it slowly. Sudden movements could scare the snake. Never try to tease a rattlesnake, chase it, or pick it up – most bites happen because people do this!

WHAT NOT TO DO

Do not cut into the bite, try to suck the poison out, or tie a tight tourniquet or bandage around the bitten body part. These things can actually make matters a lot worse.

DANGER RATING

RISK RATING: ☠ ☠ ☠
Rattlesnakes are common in many parts of the USA and other countries.

SURVIVAL RATING: 80%
Not all rattlesnake bites are deadly, and most can be treated, so you're likely to survive.

IF YOU ARE BITTEN:

Call for help to get to a hospital as soon as you can, where you can be treated with antivenom. Sit still and stay calm, and hold the bitten part lower than your heart. Moving around increases your bloodflow and makes the poison spread. Remove all watches and jewellery in case of swelling. If possible, wash the bite with soap and water.

An Eastern diamondback, one of the most dangerous species of rattlesnake.

COBRA ATTACK

Cobras are highly poisonous snakes. There are several types of cobras, all found in southern Asia and Africa. When a cobra feels threatened, it will lift up the front of its body, and spread out the ribs behind its head, forming a distinctive, wide "hood" shape. Then, the cobra may strike its prey. Cobra venom is dangerous. It kills by paralyzing the body, making it impossible to breathe. Bites can be treated with antivenom or a medical breathing machine.

DANGER RATING

RISK RATING: ☠ ☠
Cobras do not want to bite you and will only do so if cornered. Stay calm and move away.

SURVIVAL RATING: 70%
It's possible to survive most cobra bites, except in the case of the king cobra.

WHAT TO DO

IF A COBRA REARS UP:
This means it is angry or scared and may bite. Back away immediately, and keep a distance of at least the length of the snake between it and yourself. A cobra can dart its body forwards and strike suddenly.

IF YOU ARE BITTEN:
Get to a hospital as fast as possible. Stay calm, lying still and keeping the bitten body part down. Try to remember what the cobra looked like so that doctors can identify the species.

DID YOU KNOW?
Spitting cobras, which are found in Africa, can squirt venom into their victims' eyes from a distance of over 2 m (7 ft) away.

This Indian cobra is feeling threatened – stay well away!

VAMPIRE BAT

Vampire bats that suck your blood are not just found in comics and films – they really exist! There are three types of vampire bats, but only one of them attacks humans – the common vampire bat, found in Central and South America. Vampire bats feed on blood, usually from livestock, and nothing else, and they need to feed every night.

DANGER RATING

RISK RATING: ☠ ☠
Vampire bats are a risk in some South American countries.

SURVIVAL RATING: 90%
The vampire bat bite in itself is not very dangerous, but it can give you rabies. However, quick treatment can keep you safe.

The vampire bat uses its sharp front teeth to make a small, painless cut in the skin.

WHAT TO DO

PROTECT YOURSELF:
If you're in an area that has vampire bats, make sure your house, hut, or tent has no openings, and close your windows at night. Sleeping under a mosquito net will also keep bats away.

SPOT THE SIGNS:
A vampire bat's saliva contains a painkiller, so when it bites you, you don't feel it and don't wake up. It can be difficult to tell if you've been bitten. Check for any small, curved cuts or grazes on your skin.

WING WALKERS
Like other bats, vampire bats can fly, but when they get close to their victims, they land and walk, so that they can sneak up quietly. They walk by folding up their wings and using them like feet.

IF YOU THINK YOU'VE BEEN BITTEN:
Go to the hospital within 24 hours and get treated for rabies. Left untreated, rabies is likely to be fatal.

CROCODILE AND ALLIGATOR

Crocodiles and alligators are big, dangerous water reptiles with sharp teeth and strong jaws. They live in rivers, lakes, swamps, estuaries, and sometimes even in the sea. Crocodiles, found around the world, have more pointed snouts, while alligators, found mostly in the USA, have wide snouts. Both are dangerous, and they behave in similar ways.

WHAT TO DO

KNOW THE DANGERS:
In an area that has crocodiles or alligators, don't hang around near water. Don't paddle, swim, dangle your feet, or sit on the bank, even if the water looks empty. Crocs like to hide, then zoom out of the water at high speed to grab their prey.

DANGER RATING

RISK RATING: ☠ ☠ ☠
Most crocodiles and alligators prefer other foods to humans, but attacks still happen regularly.

SURVIVAL RATING: 25%
If a croc or alligator actually attacks you, you'll need luck and courage to get away.

IF YOU SEE A CROC OR ALLIGATOR:
If you're in the water, get out at once and move away. Crocs can swim faster than you. On land, run away fast. If a crocodile or alligator runs after you, keep running as fast as you can, as it will soon get tired.

IF IT CATCHES YOU:
Repeatedly punch the crocodile on the snout and face or hit it with anything in reach, and scream and shout. This may make it let go. If you get free, run away and go to a hospital, since a croc's mouth contains harmful disease germs.

TOP TIP! In cartoons, people sometimes try to wedge a croc's mouth open with a stick. Do not attempt this – crocodiles and alligators have incredibly powerful jaws and you won't succeed. A punch on the nose will work better.

KOMODO DRAGON

Dragons don't really exist – the Komodo dragon is actually a type of lizard. In fact, it's the biggest lizard in the world, growing up to 3 metres (10 feet) long. Komodo dragons live on only a few islands in Indonesia. They hunt large animals such as deer and also feed on carrion, or dead meat. They have a powerful bite that injects their prey with lethal disease bacteria. The bacteria can cause death in about two days. The dragon then comes back to feast on the dead animal.

DID YOU KNOW?

If a Komodo dragon is in danger, it can suddenly vomit up its last meal. This reduces its body weight, allowing it to run away more easily.

WHAT TO DO

IF YOU SEE A KOMODO DRAGON:

If you do see one, it will probably be at a zoo or wildlife reserve. Sometimes dragons that are kept illegally, as pets, escape – if you see one on the loose, take shelter indoors and call the police.

ON A TOURIST TRIP:

Tourists are taken on guided tours to see Komodo dragons in the wild. On a trip like this, always stay quiet and calm, and follow your guide's instructions.

IF A KOMODO DRAGON ATTACKS:

As with crocodiles and alligators, try to hit the dragon's nose and head to make it let go. Run away and have any bites treated in a hospital to kill the deadly bacteria.

DANGER RATING

RISK RATING: ☠
Komodo dragons are very rare, so you are not at great risk.

SURVIVAL RATING: 95%
Though they can be deadly, Komodo dragons don't often kill people.

If you see a Komodo in the wild, never try to feed or touch it.

FUNNEL-WEB SPIDER

The funnel-web spider is found in Australia, and it's one of the most poisonous spiders in the world. There are several species, the most dangerous being the Sydney funnel-web. Most bites happen in late summer, when male spiders are wandering around in search of a female to mate with. They may roam into a house or garage or get trapped in a shed.

WHAT TO DO

BE ON YOUR GUARD:
In eastern Australia, keep a lookout for funnel-web spiders, especially when gardening, hiking, or camping. Learn what the spiders and their webs look like so you'll know what to avoid.

IF YOU ARE BITTEN:
A funnel-web spider bite hurts! You may start to feel sick, dizzy, or tingly. Get to a hospital at once. Keep the bitten body part still. Try to wrap it in a bandage above the bite, and use a splint (a stiff stick) to stop it from moving. For example, for a bite on the hand, wrap the bandage around the arm, starting at the bite and working up to the shoulder. Then tie the splint to hold it straight. If you can, collect the spider safely and take it with you to be identified.

TOP TIP! Always check inside any boots, watering cans, containers, or clothing that has been left outdoors, before you use them. A spider could be hiding inside.

The male Sydney funnel-web spider measures about 3 cm (1.5 in) long, not including its legs.

BLACK WIDOW SPIDER

Black widow spiders have very poisonous venom. But these are small spiders, with a body length of about 1.5 centimetres (0.6 inches), and they cannot inject much venom at once.

Black widows are found in warm countries around the world. They can be killers, but in most cases being bitten by a black widow is unpleasant rather than deadly. Females are much more dangerous than males. Bites usually happen when people disturb black widow webs in woods, garages, or gardens at night, when the spiders are active.

DANGER RATING

RISK RATING: ☠ ☠ ☠
Black widow spiders are common and widespread.

SURVIVAL RATING: 95%
Most black widow bites are not fatal.

Most species of black widows are black. Females have hourglass-shaped markings or spots.

WHAT TO DO

SPIDER SENSE:
Black widows come out at night, so avoid stumbling around the garage, garden, or shed in the dark. If you see a black widow, keep your distance and give it time to scuttle away.

IF YOU ARE BITTEN:
Some people do not react much at all to black widow bites, but in most cases the bite will be painful. You should be able to see two tiny fang marks. The poison can cause muscle cramps throughout the body, stomach pain, and vomiting. If you have these symptoms, or think you have been bitten by a black widow, it's always best go to a hospital, even though you may not need antivenom. You can also treat the bite by pressing on it with ice wrapped in a cloth.

HIPPO

Few people realize just how dangerous hippos can be. They seem like slow, lumbering beasts that graze peacefully on the grass or float around in rivers. But hippos are big and powerful, have very sharp teeth, and can run surprisingly fast, reaching speeds of up to 40 kph (25 mph). In Africa, where hippos live, they have claimed hundreds of lives – far more than "fiercer" animals such as lions.

WHAT TO DO

RISK RATING: ☠ ☠
Hippos are a risk in Africa, both on land and water, but most people know how to stay safe.

SURVIVAL RATING: 60%
If a hippo decides to charge you, you'll have to run fast to get away.

Hippos spend most of the day in rivers, coming out at night to feed on grass.

UNDERSTAND HIPPOS:

Hippos are mainly vegetarians and don't want to eat people. They charge if they feel scared or if they are protecting their young. On land, don't get between a hippo and the water, for they like to feel they can reach it at all times. In a boat, be careful not to poke a swimming hippo with your oar – the hippo could upturn the boat and its occupants, or even bite it in two. Always avoid hippos at night, when they are most alert.

CHASED BY A CHARGING HIPPO:

There's no way you can fight a hippo, so start running! Hippos can run fast, but they soon get tired, so you may be able to get away. If you can, go inside a building or a large vehicle, or run among trees or rocks that will slow the hippo down. If the hippo is closing in, you may be able to gain some extra time by changing direction before it reaches you.

DID YOU KNOW?

Hippos are huge! They can grow up to 4 m (13 ft) long and can weigh up to 3,600 kg (8,000 lb) – as much as 50 grown men.

ELEPHANT

ELEPHANT RAGE

Experts think elephants may be becoming more violent and attacking humans deliberately, in return for our hunting them.

Elephants are the biggest land animals on Earth. A male African elephant can grow to over 3.5 metres (11 feet) tall and weigh 7,500 kilograms (16,500 pounds). Elephants can move fast, too – like hippos, they can run 25 mph (40 kph). So if an elephant charges or attacks, it can be deadly. Female elephants sometimes charge to protect their families, while males can enter a violent state known as "musth". Elephants are responsible for hundreds of deaths every year.

WHAT TO DO

IF AN ELEPHANT CHARGES:

Run away as fast as you can and head for the safety of a strong building, hide behind a large rock, or climb a tall tree. Running in a zigzag pattern may confuse the elephant, and if you are carrying anything, try throwing it off to one side to distract the animal. If the elephant catches you, it may trample you, crush you with its head, or spear you with its tusks. Curl up in a ball, cover your head, and try to crawl or roll to a hiding place.

IN ELEPHANT COUNTRY:

Elephants live in Africa and Asia and are a popular sight for tourists. Never approach elephants on your own – always go with a guided tour.

DANGER RATING

RISK RATING: ☠ ☠ ☠
In countries that have elephants, they are a serious danger.

SURVIVAL RATING: 60%
You can survive being chased and mauled by an elephant.

DOMESTIC DOG

For most people, dogs are loyal friends. But they are descended from wild animals, and they still have natural instincts to hunt and to defend their territory and their puppies. If a dog is angry or scared, it might attack, and because dogs have sharp teeth and strong jaws, they can be dangerous. Millions of people get bitten by dogs every year, and hundreds die from attacks.

Dogs have large, sharp teeth, useful in the wild for killing their prey.

DANGER RATING

RISK RATING:

Dogs are everywhere, and you should always regard them as a possible danger.

SURVIVAL RATING: 95%

Most people who are bitten by a dog will survive.

WHAT TO DO

TREAT DOGS WITH RESPECT:

Although dogs can be fun to pet and play with, don't do this with a dog you don't know or with one that is away from its owner. If you want to touch or stroke a dog, always ask the owner first. Stay away from dogs that are guarding their territory – for example in their garden – and from mother dogs with puppies.

SPOT THE DANGER SIGNS:

If a dog is angry, it may wag its tail very fast, prick up its ears, snarl, growl, or stare at you. Don't look the dog in the eyes, because this makes it feel threatened, and don't run away, for this will make it want to chase you. Stand up tall, stay calm, and tell the dog firmly to go away. Move slowly into a safer position, such as behind some furniture.

IF A DOG ATTACKS:

Curl up in a ball and cover your face and neck with your arms. Lie as still as you can until the dog leaves or help arrives.

DON'T FORGET RABIES!

If you ever get bitten by a dog, you should see a doctor. In many countries, aggressive dogs can be carrying rabies.

PACK OF WOLVES

Wolves are featured in fairy tales as big, bad, and dangerous, but in fact they are less dangerous than pet dogs. These hunters live in packs, and their favourite prey is a weak, sick, or old member of a herd of four-legged animals. Some think wolves avoid humans because we stand on two legs, which reminds them of a bear.

WHAT TO DO

BE WARY OF WOLVES:
Wolves often live in mountainous, forested, or cold parts of the world. Most avoid humans. If you do see wolves, stay away from them, especially if you have a pet dog with you – the wolves may see it as a threat and try to attack it. Stay close to other people.

IF WOLVES ATTACK:
When a pack of wolves finds prey, they will move downwind of their victim, then approach it in single file or spread out to surround it. If you see this happening near you, climb a tree or high rock, get inside a building or vehicle, or stand up tall and raise your arms to scare the wolves away.

A RABID WOLF:
A lone wolf might attack you if it has rabies, for this deadly disease can make animals go crazy and act aggressively. If it pounces, behave as you would for a dog attack.

DANGER RATING

RISK RATING: ☠
Though wolves can kill a human easily, they hardly ever attack people.

SURVIVAL RATING: 70%
If wolves do decide to attack, they are quite dangerous.

DID YOU KNOW?
Wolves don't howl to scare people! They mainly make this sound to call to other members of their pack, or group.

DINGO

A dingo is a type of wild dog found in Australia and Southeast Asia. Dingoes are golden-brown and fluffy and look a lot like friendly pet dogs. But most dingoes are not tame, and they can be extremely dangerous. They are sometimes found in packs, and sometimes alone. Dingoes are most likely to attack young children or to bite tourists who try to feed and play with them.

DANGER RATING

RISK RATING: ☠ ☠ ☠
In some parts of Australia, dingoes are common and a well-known risk.

SURVIVAL RATING: 95%
Very few people have died from dingo attacks, though it does happen.

A dingo is similar in size to a large pet dog.

WHAT TO DO

DINGO SENSE:

In places where dingoes are found, especially Australia, tourists often want to see them in the wild and treat them like pet dogs. Don't do this! Don't try to feed dingoes, pet them, or photograph them up close. Stay together in your group, and never let small children wander off on their own.

IF A DINGO APPROACHES YOU:

Keep an eye on the dingo (or dingoes) and try to stay facing towards it, but don't stare at the dingo since this may be interpreted as a challenge. Fold your arms, stand as tall as you can, and stay calm. Don't scream or shout at first, but if the dingo starts to attack, it may be scared off if you make a sudden loud noise.

IN A DINGO ATTACK:

Unlike some other types of dog, it is possible to scare a dingo away by shouting at it and hitting it. Use any object you may be carrying, such as a stick or an umbrella, to try to defend yourself.

TOP TIP! When camping in a dingo area, you should keep all your food, rubbish, and even supplies such as toothpaste wrapped up well and shut away, since they can attract dingoes.

HYENA

Hyenas live in Africa and Asia. They look a bit like dogs, but they have bigger, thicker, longer necks, which contain huge muscles that give hyenas incredible biting power. Their jaws are among the strongest of any animal.

Hyenas usually feed on dead animals, but one type of hyena, the spotted hyena, is a fierce hunter. If hyenas are hungry, they may attack humans. Groups of hyenas have even been known to raid villages.

A spotted hyena, the species that is most dangerous to humans.

WHAT TO DO

AVOID THE DANGER:
Hyenas are active mainly at night – don't sleep outdoors or wander around outside in the dark. Listen for whooping or cackling calls that could tell you hyenas are around. Hyenas prefer to attack the young, weak, or sick – keep these people safe.

IF YOU SEE HYENAS:
Always stay away from hyenas unless you are in a secure touring jeep with an experienced guide. If hyenas are approaching you, quickly get inside a car or building or climb a tree before they can surround you.

IF HYENAS ATTACK:
When hyenas attack people, they often lunge straight at the person's neck or head to inflict a deadly bite. You may be able to defend yourself for a few seconds by putting something between yourself and the hyena. If you don't have anything, cover your face with your arms.

DID YOU KNOW? Hyenas use their powerful jaws to munch and crunch up every bit of the animals they eat – including the bones. Most animals gnaw at a bone, but a hyena just crushes it. Even a bear can't do that.

BUFFALO

It's natural to be scared of fierce hunting animals like bears, big cats, and sharks. But would you know to be scared of a buffalo? These large animals are closely related to cows. Like cows, they wander around in herds, munching grass. But if a buffalo is angry, scared, or wounded – or if you get too close to its calf – it can be incredibly dangerous. Buffaloes can charge at high speed, goring (stabbing) their enemies with their huge horns, or trampling them flat.

WHAT TO DO

Buffaloes have huge, sharp, dangerous horns.

RESPECT THE BUFFALO:
There are several types of buffalo, but the African buffalo is the wildest and most dangerous. It is found across southern and eastern parts of the continent. If you are on a tour, always follow your guide's instructions.

IN A BUFFALO CHARGE:
If a buffalo, or a herd of buffaloes, decides to charge at you, it will move slowly at first, giving you some warning. Get inside a building or vehicle, or climb a tree if you can. If it's too late for that, your best chance is to lie down. If you stand up, the buffalo will gore you with its horns, but if you're lying down, it may run past you.

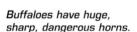

DANGER RATING

RISK RATING: ☠ ☠ ☠
In Africa, buffaloes are a well-known danger and you should always be wary of them.

SURVIVAL RATING: 80%
Buffaloes kill people every year, but if you take care, you should be safe.

A grizzly bear shows off his powerful jaws and sharp teeth.

BEAR ATTACK

Bears are big, strong, and fierce and can be very dangerous. A male grizzly bear can weigh over 270 kilograms (600 pounds) and stand over 2 metres (7 feet) tall on his hind legs.

The greatest danger comes from black bears and grizzly (or brown) bears, found in wild, mountainous areas, and polar bears, which live in and around the Arctic. However, only a handful of people each year actually die from bear attacks.

DANGER RATING

RISK RATING: ☠ ☠ ☠
Actual bear attacks are very rare, but many people do encounter bears while hiking and camping.

SURVIVAL RATING: 90%
In most bear encounters, the bear will give up and go away.

WHAT TO DO

IF YOU SEE A BEAR:
Stay at least 50 metres (150 feet) away from the bear. Keep everyone in your group close together. Don't stare at the bear or make it feel trapped. Make noise – talk, whistle, or sing. If the bear knows you're there, it will probably go away.

IF THE BEAR APPROACHES YOU:
Make a loud noise by shouting or banging pots and pans. Make yourself look bigger by waving your arms or lifting your backpack onto your head. Back away slowly, still making yourself look big.

IF THE BEAR CHARGES OR ATTACKS:
Bears often make a bluff charge, then back off. If the bear leaps on you, roll into a ball and protect your head with your arms or backpack. If the bear continues its attack, try hitting its eyes or snout.

TOP TIP! Never run away from a bear! A bear can run faster than you can – up to 48 kph (30 mph).

LION ATTACK

The lion is famous for being fierce. With his huge mane and terrifying roar, the male lion is known as the "king of the jungle". This is mostly a myth. Lions don't live in the jungle at all – they live in grasslands, usually in Africa. Although they can be dangerous, lions kill fewer people than many other wild animals. However, some lions do seem to turn against humans and start hunting them deliberately – and no lion should be considered safe.

DANGER RATING

RISK RATING: ☠ ☠
Lions are fairly rare, so lion attacks are only occasional.

SURVIVAL RATING: 40%
If you're attacked by lions, the chances are they'll win the fight.

Only male lions have the distinctive shaggy mane.

WHAT TO DO

NEVER TRUST A LION:
Lions spend most of the day sleeping. They are most active at night, but they can hunt at any time of day. If you see lions in the wild, stay inside a building or vehicle. People have been attacked when they climbed out of their jeep to take photos. Don't be fooled by a group of lions that seem to be snoozing – they will be watching you carefully and may be considering an attack.

IF LIONS ARE APPROACHING YOU:
Try not to panic and run – move backwards and get inside somewhere safe. Be careful, for lions may split up and close in from several sides.

IN AN ATTACK:
It's worth gaining some time by fighting and trying to get away. Yell for help – others may be able to scare the lion away or beat it off.

TOP TIP! If you're viewing lions from a car or jeep, keep the windows closed, and never stick your arms or head out of the vehicle!

TIGER ATTACK

The tiger is the biggest cat in the world. A male can measure up to 12 feet (3.5 m) long from nose to tail. That's as long as a car! Tigers are also immensely strong and can cover as much as 30 feet (9 m) in one leap.

Tigers live in India, China, and other parts of Asia, mainly in grassy or forested areas. They usually hunt wild animals such as wild deer or pigs, but they do sometimes attack humans if food is scarce.

DANGER RATING

RISK RATING: ☠ ☠
Tigers are very rare, and they do not normally think of humans as food.

SURVIVAL RATING: 30%
If a tiger does decide to attack you, it's not good news!

Avoid travelling alone in tiger country!

WHAT TO DO

IF YOU SEE A TIGER:
At first, keep still and quiet.
Tigers are more likely to spot you if you move. Wait until the tiger has gone before making your way to safety.

IF A TIGER IS STALKING YOU:
If possible, get into a hiding place such as a vehicle, a hut, or a narrow space between rocks, where the tiger won't be able to reach you. Otherwise, turn to face the tiger, and look as tall and brave as you can. This puts most tigers off, because they like to take their prey by surprise.

IF THE TIGER POUNCES:
If a tiger is leaping through the air at you, figure out where it will land and run to one side, heading for any rocks, trees, or other shelter. If the tiger grabs you, your only hope is for someone to shoot it, beat it off, or scare it away.

PUMA

The puma – also known as the mountain lion, cougar, or catamount – is a big cat found in North, Central, and South America. It has a plain golden-brown or reddish-brown colour and is around 76 centimetres (2.5 feet) tall and 2.3 metres (7 feet) long from its nose to the tip of its tail. Although they are not as big as lions and tigers, pumas can be dangerous, especially to children. They sometimes attack hikers, walkers, and villagers in mountain areas, forests, and deserts.

DANGER RATING

RISK RATING: 💀💀
Pumas are not likely to attack; they do not usually see humans as food.

SURVIVAL RATING: 70%
Most people can survive a puma encounter, but children are at serious risk if they are attacked.

WHAT TO DO

TAKE CARE IN PUMA COUNTRY:
Watch out for pumas in mountain, scrubland, and forest areas, especially in the western United States and Canada. Never go near a puma kitten or den – a mother puma will defend her babies fiercely.

IF YOU SEE A PUMA:
Don't panic. Look the puma in the eye and back away slowly. Stand tall, raise your arms, and shout loudly to scare the puma. Don't bend down or turn your back to the puma, because this may encourage it to pounce.

IF THE PUMA POUNCES:
Defend your neck and head; the puma will try to bite you here. Fight back, yell, and try to beat the puma off.

Pumas like to jump on prey from trees or high rocks, so watch out!

DID YOU KNOW?

Pumas have very large, powerful back legs and are brilliant at jumping. They can leap as high as 5 m (16 ft) straight up or 10 m (33 ft) horizontally.

WILD BOAR

A male wild boar shows off his tusks.

The wild boar is the untamed version of the domestic pig. Pigs themselves can be dangerous, but wild boar are even scarier – they have sharp tusks and teeth and will charge to defend themselves. They can reach up to 2 metres (7 feet) in length and weigh up to twice as much as a man. They are found in many parts of the world, including Australia, Europe, Asia, and South America, mostly in forest areas.

WHAT TO DO

BEWARE OF THE BOARS:
Take care in forests if you know wild boars are around, especially at night when they are most active. You are at greater risk if you have a dog, because it may disturb wild boars and make them angry.

DANGER RATING

RISK RATING: ☠ ☠
Wild boars are getting more common, but they won't charge if you leave them alone.

SURVIVAL RATING: 95%
You'll almost certainly survive, but boar attacks can sometimes be deadly due to loss of blood.

IF YOU SEE WILD BOARS:
Wild boars may be found alone or in groups of about 20, made up of mothers and their young. Steer clear of them, especially if you see babies. If boars are about to charge, they will face you, snorting and grunting. Move away fast if this happens.

IF A WILD BOAR CHARGES:
Male boars charge with their heads down, then slash with their large tusks. Females charge with their mouths open, then bite you. Your best strategy is to climb a tree, or run away as fast as you can.

TOP TIP! A boar injured by a hunter or hit by a car can be furious and highly dangerous. If you see one, run away at once.

HORSE

Humans have been training and riding horses for thousands of years. They are among the most important domestic animals in the world. Horses are big and strong, and since they have such close contact with humans, it's no surprise that there are thousands of horse-related accidents every year. A fall from a horse can be very dangerous, especially if you're not wearing a helmet.

Horses may kick and struggle, rear up, or run wildly if agitated.

WHAT TO DO

MAKE HORSES FEEL SAFE:
Horses may be big, but they are easily scared. Most accidents happen when horses feel trapped or threatened. Always treat horses respectfully and calmly: Never tease them, make them jump, or creep up on them from behind. Don't stand behind a horse or it may kick you, and don't block a horse's path. It's best to stay away from them, unless you know them well or the owner is there.

SPOT THE WARNING SIGNS:
If a horse lays its ears flat against its head, or tosses its head, that may mean it is angry and about to kick or bite.

IF A HORSE RUNS YOU DOWN:
A panicking horse may knock you down or gallop over you. If you fall under a horse, curl up and cover your head – the horse doesn't want to hurt you and will try to avoid you.

TOP TIP! If you have a riding helmet, wear it all the time you are around horses, not just when you're riding. It could protect your head from an unexpected kick.

CHARGING BULL

A bullfighter dodges a bull, using a red cape to distract it.

DANGER RATING

RISK RATING: 💀 💀
As long as you leave bulls alone, an attack is unlikely.

SURVIVAL RATING: 90%
Bulls do kill people, especially farmers and bullfighters, but it's not common.

A bull is a male cow. Bulls, especially older ones, are often kept on their own in fields. They can be very large and can run fast, so a charging bull can be deadly. As well as chasing and trampling, it can use its horns to gore or throw its victim.

In bullfighting, people tease and taunt a bull. Bulls sometimes kill bullfighters, but the bulls are far more likely to be killed. Bulls will not usually attack you unless you scare them or enter their territory.

WHAT TO DO

DON'T GO THERE:
In the countryside, don't go into any field that has a bull in it – even if the bull is far away. If a field looks empty, check it carefully to be sure.

DANGER SIGNS:
If a bull is angry, it may arch its back, lower its head and sweep it from side to side, and paw at the ground with its hooves. Move away, keeping an eye on the bull, and get to safety as soon as you can.

IF A BULL CHARGES AT YOU:
If you're a long way from safety, the bull will catch up with you. Take off your jacket or top and wave it to one side. As the bull gets closer, throw it away. The bull should run towards it.

RED RAG TO A BULL

According to folklore, bulls are driven mad by the colour red. This isn't true – bulls are colour-blind. A moving object of any colour can make it want to charge.

SCORPION

Scorpions are related to spiders. They are usually quite small, ranging from 1.3 centimetres (0.5 inches) to 20 centimetres (8 inches) long, and have eight legs. They have two pincers and a long tail with a stinger at the end. There are over a thousand different species of scorpion, and most are not dangerous. But a few have very poisonous stingers that can occasionally kill a human.

WHAT TO DO

SCORPION SAFETY:

Scorpions are nocturnal (active at night) so if you're in an area that has dangerous scorpions, sleep under a mosquito net. Check your bed for scorpions before you get in. In the morning, shake out shoes, bags, and clothing in case a scorpion has crept inside.

DANGER RATING

RISK RATING: ☠ ☠ ☠
Scorpions prefer to avoid humans, but they are common and will sting if picked up or trodden on.

SURVIVAL RATING: 95%
There's usually time to get to a hospital, so most people survive even dangerous scorpion stings.

IF YOU FIND A SCORPION:

Leave scorpions alone and give them space to scuttle away. You can sweep a scorpion out of a house gently with a broom, but never pick one up. If a scorpion crawls onto your hand or foot, keep the body part flat and shake the scorpion off.

IF A SCORPION STINGS YOU:

If the scorpion is not dangerous, only the area around the sting will hurt. If you start to ache all over, feel sick or dizzy, or have trouble breathing, head for a hospital. If a scorpion stings a small child, or someone who is already unwell, take them to a hospital to get checked out.

The yellow scorpion, found in Brazil.

DID YOU KNOW? A scorpion cannot harm itself with its sting. It is not affected by its own poison.

KILLER BEES

Honeybees are found all over the world. They help humans by pollinating flowers and making honey. Although they can sting, they usually don't, and for most people a single bee sting is painful but not dangerous.

However, in the 1950s, scientists tried to breed a new type of honeybee that would make extra honey. Instead, they accidentally created an extra-aggressive breed, known as "killer" bees. They are now found in South and Central America, and the southern USA. These bees do not have a worse sting, but they are easily annoyed and often attack in a swarm, which can be deadly.

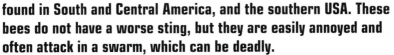

Killer bees are a type of honeybee, and look just like other honeybees.

DANGER RATING

RISK RATING: ☠ ☠
Killer bees are dangerous, but scientists are working on reducing their numbers and their aggressive tendencies.

SURVIVAL RATING: 90%
Keep a cool head, and you'll probably be able to escape.

WHAT TO DO

DON'T ANNOY THE BEES:
Killer bees are annoyed by people disturbing their nests, sudden movements, and loud noises. Using loud tools such as chain saws often triggers attacks.

IF KILLER BEES CHASE YOU:
Run as fast as you can and head for a building, a car, or anywhere you can shut yourself inside. Use your clothing to cover as much of your head and face as possible. Don't panic or scream, and don't run into a crowd of people. Don't jump into water, either – you'll have to come up to breathe, and the bees will be waiting.

BEE ALLERGIES Some people are allergic to bee stings. If someone gets stung by a bee and then has trouble breathing, a swollen face or tongue, or collapses, get them to a hospital at once.

CHIMPANZEE

You might think of chimpanzees as cute and cuddly – but you'd be wrong. Some chimpanzees are friendly, but others can be very dangerous.

In the wild, groups of chimps hunt smaller animals such as monkeys. In captivity, chimps have been known to attack people for no obvious reason. A chimp is only about 1 metre (3 feet) tall, but it weighs as much as a human, and is up to five times stronger.

A chimpanzee has sharp teeth and a dangerous bite, as well as incredibly strong arms and hands.

DANGER RATING

RISK RATING: ☠
You're unlikely to meet a chimp, except in a secure zoo.

SURVIVAL RATING: 40%
If chimps do decide to attack, it's hard to escape.

WHAT TO DO

TREAT CHIMPS WITH RESPECT:

Even at a zoo, where chimpanzees are safely enclosed, don't annoy them. Don't tease them, throw things, or knock on the glass – just in case they can get out. If you see chimps in the wild, keep clear of them and try not to stare. Don't leave small children alone in chimp areas, or let them go near chimps. If you know someone who has a pet chimp, it's best to keep your distance from it, even if it seems friendly.

IF CHIMPS ATTACK:

If a chimp is coming towards you and trying to attack you, look down and avoid making eye contact. If it attacks, curl up and protect your face, stomach, and head. Call for help so that a zookeeper or park warden can try to save you.

DID YOU KNOW?

In the 1960s, scientist Jane Goodall, famous for her studies of chimps, found out that they are hunters and eat meat as well as other foods. Before this, most people thought chimps were vegetarian.

MOSQUITO

A mosquito is a small buzzing insect, a member of the fly family. It is also the most dangerous animal in the world. Mosquitoes are more dangerous than sharks, bears, tigers, hippos, crocodiles, jellyfish, dogs, and killer bees – all rolled together! Mosquitoes suck blood, and when they bite, they spread deadly diseases, including malaria and yellow fever. Although most of these diseases can be treated, they often strike in poor areas where people cannot afford medicine, so the death toll is very high. Mosquito bites cause around three million deaths each year.

WHAT TO DO

GUARD AGAINST MOSQUITOES:
Dangerous mosquitoes are mainly found in hot, tropical parts of the world, including Africa, southern Asia, and South America. If you are in these areas, you can take special medicines that help prevent malaria. You should also wear insect repellent and cover your arms and legs, especially in the hours of darkness when mosquitoes are active. At night, sleep under a mosquito net.

BLOOD SUCKERS

Mosquitoes don't actually need blood for food. Like butterflies, they feed on fruit and flower nectar. Only the females suck blood, which they need to help them make their eggs.

IF YOU CATCH MALARIA:
The symptoms of malaria include headaches, feeling very hot and very cold, and feeling sick, dizzy, or tingly. If you feel ill in a tropical country, see a doctor.

A mosquito's body fills up with blood as it sucks from its human host.

SHARK ATTACK

Few things are scarier than the thought of being chased through the water by a terrifying shark, but this image comes mainly from films. In fact, attacks are rare, and sharks are less dangerous than many other animals, including elephants, hippos, or even bees. Most sharks only attack humans because they mistake them for prey, such as seals and penguins.

DANGER RATING

RISK RATING: ☠ ☠
Fewer than 100 shark attacks a year are reported around the world. Half of all shark attacks are reported by surfers.

SURVIVAL RATING: 90%
Despite their fearsome reputation, you will probably escape even if a shark does bite you.

WHAT TO DO

DON'T BE A TARGET:
Don't swim or surf at night, avoid deep water and river mouths, and don't go into murky, frothy water, where a shark could mistake you for a meal. Don't wear anything silvery or sparkly that might look like fish scales.

IF A SHARK APPROACHES YOU:
Keep calm and swim for land. If the shark circles you or bumps you with its nose, stay still and upright, so that it won't think you're a seal. If you're with others, cling together to make a big shape that the shark will not want to approach.

IF A SHARK ATTACKS YOU:
Hit the snout or eyes, or hit it with something, such as a snorkel, to make the shark let you go. Shout for help and try to get ashore, then seek medical help.

DID YOU KNOW? The great white shark is widely feared, but is not the most aggressive shark. The bull shark, though smaller, is more common and more likely to attack humans.

PIRANHA SHOAL

Piranhas are fish that live in rivers in South America, such as the Amazon. They have a deadly reputation. In adventure films they hunt in shoals, attacking large animals, such as cows and humans, who have wandered into the water. They are said to bite all the flesh from their victim's bones, churning up the water in a violent "feeding frenzy".

The truth is, they rarely eat people. Piranhas are meat eaters, and they do swim in groups and hunt prey, such as birds, that fall into the water. At certain times of year, however, such as the dry season, they can be very dangerous to humans.

DANGER RATING

RISK RATING: ☠ ☠
If you're in South America, piranhas are a risk, but only a small one.

SURVIVAL RATING: 95%
Few people die from a piranha attack, but these fish give a nasty bite!

Most piranhas are only about 25 cm (10 in) long, but they are aggressive.

WHAT TO DO

PIRANHA SAFETY:
If you are in South America, avoid going into rivers during the dry season, when the water level falls and hungry piranhas crowd together in schools. If you are swimming, don't splash around – it could make piranhas think you're an injured animal. Don't go into the water if you have an illness or injury. Most people who are attacked by piranhas are thought to get into trouble in the water first and start panicking, attracting the fish.

TOP TIP! Stay away from piranhas on the bank when they have been caught as food. They may still be alive and have a powerful bite – a piranha can bite your finger off.

IF YOU SEE PIRANHAS:
Leave the water if you see piranhas, or if you are warned of sightings. If you are attacked, your best chance is to get out of the water as fast as you can.

STINGRAY

Rays are a type of fish related to sharks. They "fly" along underwater by flapping their wide fins. Stingrays are a group of rays that have a long, sharp, venomous stinger in their tails. If a stingray feels threatened, it can flip its stinger upwards suddenly. If you stand on a stingray as it lies on the seabed, or if you swim over the top of one too closely, the stinger could stab you and inject you with poison. The sting is painful, but not usually dangerous.

A southern stingray photographed off the Cayman Islands.

WHAT TO DO

TAKE CARE IN THE WATER:
Stingrays are found in warm, tropical parts of the world, usually in the sea, close to the shore, but also in some rivers. Keep a lookout for stingrays when you are swimming, paddling, snorkelling, or diving.

IF YOU GET STUNG:
Most stings are on the feet or hands. Go back to the shore, and try to get to a hospital for treatment, as parts of the stinger may have broken off under your skin. You can relieve the pain with warm water. Bandage the wound to stop bleeding, if necessary. If you have been stung in the face or body, this could be more dangerous. Do not pull the stinger out, as this could make the wound bleed dangerously. The poison does not usually kill, but the stinger wound can be serious.

TOP TIP! Stingrays often lie flat on the seabed and can be difficult to see. But you can avoid treading on them by shuffling your feet forward through the sand. This will allow a stingray to feel you coming, and it will move away.

SEA SNAKE

Most snakes live on land, but there is a group of snakes that swim in the sea. They look like other snakes, except that the ends of their tails are flattened, like oars, to help them swim. Most sea snakes are very poisonous – their venom is much stronger than that of most land snakes. They usually leave divers and swimmers alone, but they can inflict a deadly bite, especially if they get caught in a fishing net or washed ashore, where someone might tread on them.

DANGER RATING

RISK RATING: ☠
Unless you work on a fishing boat, you will probably not encounter a sea snake.

SURVIVAL RATING: 90%
Even if they bite, sea snakes do not always inject venom, and bites can be treated with antivenom.

WHAT TO DO

IF YOU SEE A SEA SNAKE:
You might see a sea snake while scuba diving or snorkelling, or on the beach, if it has been washed ashore after a storm. Wherever it is, don't touch it. Move away. In the water, sea snakes are curious and often follow divers to look at their equipment. They probably won't bite, but it's best to get away from them if you can.

IF A SEA SNAKE BITES YOU:
You may not feel the bite at first, but if venom has been injected, the poison will soon give you a headache and make you feel sick. Your muscles will start to feel stiff and painful. Gradually, you will feel more and more tired, and it might become hard to breathe. Seek help. There is an antivenom that can stop the worst effects of the poison.

CLOSED NOSE

Sea snakes can't breathe underwater – they have to come to the surface for air. While diving in the sea, they can close their nostrils to keep water out.

BOX JELLYFISH

The box jellyfish is the world's deadliest jellyfish. There are no exact figures, but it is estimated to cause at least 50 deaths per year, mainly in Australia and southeast Asia.

The box jellyfish is large, with a cube-shaped top part up to 25 centimetres (10 inches) across, and stinging tentacles up to 3 metres (10 feet) long. It hunts shrimps and crabs and probably has little interest in humans, but if a swimmer gets caught in its tentacles, it will sting. This jellyfish's sting scars the skin and can stop the heart.

DANGER RATING

RISK RATING: ☠ ☠ ☠ ☠
In Australian and Asian waters, the box jellyfish is common.

SURVIVAL RATING: 70%
Box jellyfish stings are not always deadly, and there are treatments and an antivenom.

WHAT TO DO

STAY SAFE:

In areas that have box jellyfish, don't swim in the sea during jellyfish season (usually the wet season, from October to March). There are often signposts to warn of jellyfish danger. If you do want or need to swim, don't go alone. You can also protect yourself by covering your skin with light clothing, a wetsuit, or a "stingersuit".

DID YOU KNOW?

Some jellyfish stings can be treated by pouring urine onto them! But remember, this doesn't work for box jellyfish stings.

IF YOU ARE STUNG:

A box jellyfish sting is incredibly painful. Yell for help, and call an ambulance. Pour vinegar on the sting (dangerous beaches have a supply of vinegar for this purpose). If the tentacles are stuck to your skin, pick them off with a stick. Try to stay calm while you wait for medical help.

BLUE-RINGED OCTOPUS

The "beak" of a blue-ringed octopus can penetrate a wetsuit.

Compared to most octopuses, the blue-ringed octopus is tiny – small enough to sit in your hand. Yet it it is one of the most dangerous of all sea creatures, with a venomous bite that can kill a human. Its poison works by paralyzing you so that you can't breathe. There is no antivenom – the only treatment is to help the victim breathe until the venom has cleared from his or her body.

DANGER RATING

RISK RATING: ☠ ☠
Blue-ringed octopuses don't want to bite you – they only will if you touch them or tread on them.

SURVIVAL RATING: 90%
You can survive a bite as long as you know you've been bitten and act fast.

WHAT TO DO

DON'T TOUCH:
Blue-ringed octopuses are found around Australia and in the western Pacific region, usually in rock pools or close to the shore. Never touch any small octopus you find on the beach – even if it doesn't have blue rings. They can change colour to blend in with their surroundings, and the blue-ringed octopus's rings only appear when it is alarmed.

IF YOU ARE BITTEN:
You will need help to survive a blue-ringed octopus bite, so don't go to the beach alone! The bite may be painless, but you will soon start to feel numb around the mouth and find it difficult to breathe. Someone must call an ambulance immediately. While you wait for the ambulance, lie down and keep the bitten body part still. Your friends should give you mouth-to-mouth resuscitation.

HUMAN

Since humans arrived on Earth we have built billions of buildings, roads, and railways, and all kinds of transportation devices to get us from A to B. Usually, of course, these things are safe and useful,

DANGERS

but they can be dangerous. Here you can find out what to do if your parachute doesn't open, your ship sinks, or you're trapped in a burning building, a broken cable car, or a sunken submarine.

ON A SINKING SHIP

A large ship or ferry is a very safe place to be. Like a plane, it's safer than a car, a bicycle, or walking around on foot. But any ship can sink – if it hits an iceberg, for example, or gets flooded by a giant wave. To be sure of staying safe, you need to stay calm and listen carefully.

In 1952, Captain Henrik Carlsen stayed with his battered cargo ship, the Flying Enterprise, *for seven days.*

DANGER RATING

RISK RATING: ☠ ☠
Ships are very safe, but a few do sink each year around the world.

SURVIVAL RATING: 95%
Safety equipment and strategies are designed to keep you as safe as possible if your ship sinks.

TOP TIP! If you do get wet, take your wet clothes off and wrap up in something dry – even if it's just an old coat. Wet clothes will make you lose heat very fast.

WHAT TO DO

IF YOUR SHIP IS SINKING:
Obey the crew's instructions – they are trained in what to do if the ship sinks. They will send for help and arrange for everyone to board a lifeboat. Meanwhile, dress in warm clothes and put on your life jacket.

ABANDONING SHIP:
Don't panic and start fighting for a place on a lifeboat! There will be space for everyone. If you are able-bodied and strong, help children, the disabled, and the elderly to put their life jackets on and get into a lifeboat. Get in carefully yourself and hang on tight!

IN THE LIFEBOAT:
As a ship goes under, it can suck things down with it. So once a lifeboat is full, it should move as far away from the ship as possible. Stay sitting down, and huddle together keep warm.

SUNKEN SUBMARINE

Being deep underwater is dangerous for two main reasons. First, of course, we can't breathe underwater, so those in a submarine or submersible (a kind of minisubmarine) rely on the air supply they take with them. Second, the deeper you go, the more water pressure pushes in on you. In deep oceans, the pressure is so great that it can squash you to death in an instant.

WHAT TO DO

SEND AN SOS:
Unless your submarine is very badly damaged, you should be able to radio a message to rescuers on land, giving them your position.

SAVE OXYGEN:
While you wait, you need to do as little as possible. The less you do, the less of your air supply you'll use up. Sit or lie down, keep warm and talk quietly, read, or sleep.

HOLD OUT HOPE:
Being trapped in a small space is frightening and might make you panic. You need to keep your spirits up and stay calm. Try to comfort and reassure one another, talk about plans for the future, and sing songs to pass the time.

DANGER RATING

RISK RATING: ☠
Not many people will find themselves in this situation.

SURVIVAL RATING: 40%
Survival depends on being rescued, which may not happen in time.

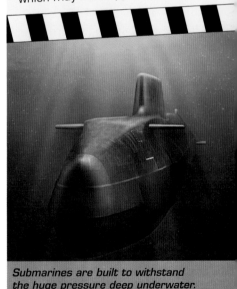

Submarines are built to withstand the huge pressure deep underwater.

ROBOT RESCUE

In 2005, a Russian minisubmarine became trapped underwater when its propellers were caught in fishing nets. Rescuers used remote-controlled robot vehicles to cut the sub free. The seven crew members were saved after three days underwater, with just six hours of air to spare.

TRAPPED IN A SINKING CAR

When you travel by car, you're shut inside a strong, protective box, and strapped in for safety. But if your car lands in water, these safety features become dangerous. The car will sink, and you need to get out quickly. Don't think about taking stuff with you. Concentrate on making sure everyone gets out of the car before it goes under.

DANGER RATING

RISK RATING: Driving into deep water isn't very common, though driving over ice increases the risk.

SURVIVAL RATING: 70%
It is often possible to get out, but this is a very dangerous situation.

WHAT TO DO

UNDO YOUR SEAT BELT:
If your car veers off the road and hits water, you'll need your seat belt to lessen the impact. But as soon as the car comes to a stop, make sure everyone's seat belt is undone. Check baby and child seats, too.

OPEN A WINDOW:
The water pressing against the car will make it almost impossible to open the doors. Instead, open the windows fully and climb out. If the windows are electric and aren't working, you'll have to break the glass with your foot or a heavy object. Take care to avoid the broken glass.

IF YOU CAN'T OPEN THE WINDOWS:
Wait inside the car as it fills up with water. Once the car is nearly filled with water, and the air is almost gone, take a deep breath and hold it. You should be able to open a door and escape.

TOP TIP! Once you're free from the car, everyone should cling together and tread water until you have your breath back. Then you can start to yell for help or swim for the shore.

Serious danger: This car has turned upside down in rough water.

BRAKE FAILURE

Cars on motorways drive at high speed. The faster you are going, the longer it will take to stop.

Brakes are there to slow down and stop cars, trucks, buses, and other vehicles. You rely on the brakes to stop at traffic lights, avoid hazards, and turn corners. If your brakes don't work and you can't stop, you're in serious danger of a crash — so all drivers should know what to do. Even if you can't drive yet, it might be worth remembering!

WHAT TO DO

CHECK THE PEDAL:
Often, when a driver can't get the brakes to work, it's because a water bottle, a box of tissues, or some other junk is stuck under the brake pedal. Try to sweep under the pedal with your foot to remove any blockage. Keep trying the brake pedal, for it may start working again. Right away, make sure everyone has their seat belts on.

STEER TO SAFETY:
You need to get away from other cars you could crash into. Signal and move carefully to the side of the road, watching out for pedestrians.

FIND SOMETHING TO SLOW YOU DOWN:
If you are not going too fast — less than 60 kph (40 mph) — use the hand brake to slow you down. You can also try running the car along the edge of the curb or steering it up a hill, if you can do so safely. On country roads, drive off the road onto flat grass or dirt.

TOP TIP! Once you've stopped, don't sit in the car — get everyone out and move them to a safe place while you wait for help.

PARACHUTE FAILURE

DANGER RATING

RISK RATING: ☠
Not many people go parachuting, and if you do, your parachute will almost certainly work.

SURVIVAL RATING: 95%
Stay calm and use your reserve chute, and all should be well.

In the early days of parachute jumping, parachutes failed to open and got tangled up quite often. But modern parachutes are very safe and hardly ever go wrong. If yours does, you will still have a reserve parachute to rely on.

WHAT TO DO

IF YOUR PARACHUTE DOESN'T OPEN:
Don't panic. Take a moment to remember your training, and follow the procedures you have been taught for using your reserve parachute.

IF THE RESERVE CHUTE FAILS, TOO:
This is very unlikely, but it could happen. It is obviously not good news, but people have been known to survive such falls. You may be able to slow yourself down a little by spreading out your arms and legs. You are more likely to survive if you land in bushes or trees, in snow, or on soft, ploughed soil.

HITCH A RIDE:
If you have problems while skydiving, you might be able to link on to another skydiver and use his or her parachute. You will have to tie yourselves together, and may be injured while landing.

DID YOU KNOW? Some parachutes have a safety system that can sense if you are close to the ground and falling fast. The reserve chute will open automatically.

STUCK IN A CABLE CAR

DANGER RATING

RISK RATING: ☠ ☠
Cable car catastrophes are pretty rare.

SURVIVAL RATING: 80%
Usually, the car is simply stuck, and you will be rescued.

A cable car soars over Fraser River Canyon in Canada.

Cable cars carry tourists, skiers, and mountaineers up and down mountain slopes. Passengers travel in a hanging car, or a smaller "gondola", which moves up and down a long cable. There are thousands of cable car systems all over the world, and they rarely go wrong. However, cable car accidents can sometimes happen.

CABLE CAR CRASH

A cable car crashed in the Austrian village of Soelden in 2005 after a helicopter passing overhead accidently dropped its cargo of concrete.

WHAT TO DO

IF YOUR CABLE CAR STOPS:
Don't do anything! Don't panic, run around, or lean out of the windows. Never try to climb out and escape. Sit down – on the floor if there are no seats – and stay calm. You can call for help on a mobile phone, but chances are, the cable car control centre will know what has happened.

IN HIGH WINDS:
Cable cars can get stuck because of strong winds. In this situation, the car may be blown and shaken about. Stay seated and hold on to something fixed if you can. If the car slides down the cable towards another car, or even falls off the cable, hold on tight, as the impact will shake you even more.

IN A BURNING BUILDING

Every year, thousands of people around the world die in fires in their homes or in other buildings. Some fires are started deliberately, but they often start by accident, too. Fires can be caused by cigarettes, candles or stoves left burning, or electrical faults. Even fires that seem small can grow very fast and quickly become dangerous.

WHAT TO DO

IF YOU SEE A FIRE:
Back away from the fire and leave the room, closing the door. Everyone should leave the building. If there is a fire alarm, set it off on your way out. Move away from the building, then call the fire brigade.

IF YOU ARE TRAPPED IN A BURNING BUILDING:
Move away from the flames, closing doors behind you to slow down the spread of the fire. If you can use a phone safely, call the fire brigade. Go to a room with a window, open the window if you can, and wave and call for help. Don't climb out unless you are close to the ground. If fire or smoke gets into the room, stay beside the window and lie on the floor, as the heat and smoke will rise.

DANGER RATING

RISK RATING: ☠ ☠ ☠ ☠
Fire is a common danger and can affect any building. Smoke alarms save lives every year – get one.

SURVIVAL RATING: 90%
Staying calm, calling for help, and getting out fast will give you a very good chance of survival.

TOP TIP!
If you're stuck in a building that's on fire, it may seem like a good idea to break the windows, but try to avoid this. The glass could fall down onto rescuers and survivors on the ground and cause terrible injuries.

BROKEN POWER LINE

In most places, power lines carry electricity high above our heads. The high-voltage electricity is dangerous, but normally way out of reach. However, high winds, an ice storm, an earthquake, or sometimes even a helicopter or aeroplane accident, can cause power lines to break and come snaking to the ground. They may still be live with electricity and can be very dangerous indeed.

WHAT TO DO

IF YOU SEE A FALLEN POWER LINE:

First, stay away from it and don't touch it. Sometimes broken power lines shoot out sparks and snake around, so you must keep away. Even if the power line is still, and looks dead, leave it alone just in case.

IF A POWER LINE FALLS ON YOUR CAR:

The electricity could flow through the metal parts of the car. Stay inside, don't touch the car doors, and call for help.

DANGER RATING

RISK RATING: ☠ ☠
Power lines are usually only a danger during severe storms.

SURVIVAL RATING: 95%
Get away from the line, and you'll be safe.

IF THE POWER LINE TOUCHES SOMEONE:

You need to get the power line off them, but don't touch the line or the person yourself. Use a wooden or plastic object, such as a stick or traffic cone, to push the power line away. Then drag the person to safety and call an ambulance.

In July 2005, Hurricane Dennis brought down electricity pylons all over the island of Cuba, making it very dangerous to move in the wet streets.

FALLEN DOWN A MINE SHAFT

The entrance to an abandoned mine shaft in Somerset, England.

DANGER RATING

RISK RATING: ☠ ☠
Mine shafts are very dangerous, b
you are quite unlikely to fall into on

SURVIVAL RATING: 30%
Deep mine shaft falls are
often deadly.

A mine shaft is a deep, narrow hole in the ground, leading to an underground mine. At large, working mines, the entrances to mine shafts are surrounded by buildings and safety fences, so they are not usually dangerous. The biggest danger comes from abandoned mines in the countryside, especially small ones that were dug a long time ago.

WHAT TO DO
IF YOU FALL INTO A MINE SHAFT:
Many abandoned mine shafts are overgrown with bushes – so if you feel yourself falling, you might be able to grab at plants to drag yourself out. If you do fall down, protect your head with your arms, and hope it's not deep.

AT THE BOTTOM:
If you're awake, that's a good sign. Moving slowly and carefully, as you may be injured, try to get to one side of the shaft, so that you are not under the entrance. That way,

if anyone else falls in, they won't land on you. Rescuers might also dislodge rocks as they enter the shaft to find you. Yell for help, or use a mobile phone to call for help.

BEWARE OF WATER
Some mine shafts have pools of water at the bottom. If there is water, try to move away from it.

HOW DEEP?
People who fall down mine shafts typically fall about 20 m (60–70 ft). However, some mine shafts are much deeper – 100 m (330 ft) deep, or more. That's like falling off a 30-storey building.

TRAPPED IN A GRAIN SILO

Grain might not seem all that scary, but serious accidents can happen on farms when large amounts of grain are being stored, transported, or poured from one container into another.

A grain silo, or grain bin, is a huge grain container, usually several storeys high. If you are inside one, you can get trapped. Moving grain can suck you down and suffocate you.

DANGER RATING

RISK RATING: ☠ ☠
This is only a major risk on farms. Stay away from silos to be safe.

SURVIVAL RATING: 50%
When grain silo accidents happen, they're often serious.

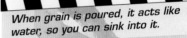

When grain is poured, it acts like water, so you can sink into it.

WHAT TO DO

STAY AWAY:
First of all, never go near grain silos, grain bins, or grain transporters of any kind – unless you are the farmer and know what you are doing.

IF YOU FALL INTO GRAIN:
If the grain is not moving, you should be able to stand on it without sinking. Stay near the walls, because a "bridge" or crust of grain can form in the middle of the silo, covering a gap below. You could fall in and get covered with grain. Keep calm and call for help.

IF YOU SINK UNDER THE GRAIN:
Grain that is being poured or moved can suck you under and hold you tight. You can also get covered in grain if you fall through a grain bridge, or if a heap of grain collapses on you. If this happens, stay calm and hold your arms in front of your face to make a breathing space as you sink.

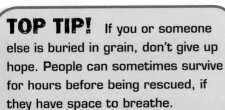

TOP TIP! If you or someone else is buried in grain, don't give up hope. People can sometimes survive for hours before being rescued, if they have space to breathe.

BRIDGE COLLAPSE

Bridges are designed to stay up. Scientists, engineers, and architects calculate very carefully how strong and what shape and size a bridge has to be, and what materials to use. But it can go wrong. A mistake in the plans or in the work, unexpected freak weather, too much weight on the bridge, or damage caused by age can all lead to a bridge collapse.

DANGER RATING

RISK RATING: ☠
Bridges collapse now and again, but there's only a very small chance you'll be involved.

SURVIVAL RATING: 70%
Bridges often fall apart quite slowly, giving people a chance to escape.

In 2007, a bridge collapsed in Nanhai, China, after a boat crashed into it.

WHAT TO DO

AVOID BRIDGE BUILDING SITES:
If a bridge is going to go wrong, it often does so at an early stage, during the building work. Avoid going near or under bridges that are being built, just in case.

IF A BRIDGE STARTS TO WOBBLE OR CREAK:
Before a bridge actually collapses, there may be several warning signs. It might creak, wobble, sway, bend, or crack. If you see or hear any of these things, get off the bridge immediately, or move out from under it. People have survived bridge collapses by leaving their cars and running off bridges. Based on the traffic, you'll have to decide if this is a good idea, or if you can get off the bridge more quickly in a vehicle.

IF THE BRIDGE FALLS:
If you're on foot as the bridge falls, hold on tight – cling to the bridge railing or cable, since it may stay attached. If you're in a vehicle, make sure your seat belt is buckled and bend forward to shelter from impact and flying glass.

TOP TIP! After you land on the ground or in water, move away from the bridge fast, because more vehicles and debris may fall on you.

PLANE CRASH

Many people don't like flying. But did you know that planes are incredibly safe and crash very rarely? You're safer on a plane than you are in a car, or even in your house. Even when planes crash, most passengers usually survive. Some plane accidents happen on the ground, and a lot of the passengers escape. Others happen when the plane goes wrong in mid-air, but the pilot may be able to make a crash landing.

This plane overshot the runway and crashed in Toronto in 2005. It caught fire, but all 309 passengers survived.

DANGER RATING

RISK RATING: ☠

Your chance of being in a plane crash is very small indeed.

SURVIVAL RATING: 90%

It might seem incredible, but over 90% of people involved in plane accidents do survive.

WHAT TO DO

BRACE! BRACE!

If the pilot or crew on a plane tell you to "Brace!" it means you should lean forward, with your head either resting on your knees or leaning against the seat in front. In a crash, this position helps to keep you still and avoid flying debris.

GET OUT FAST:

Always listen to the crew's instructions. Once the plane has come to a stop, get out, since the plane may catch fire. Undo your seat belt (remember it does not work like a car seat belt) and head for the nearest exit. If the plane is already on fire, crawling along the floor will help keep you away from the heat, smoke, and fumes.

ONCE YOU'RE OUT:

Follow the crew's instructions for getting down a safety ramp. Check yourself for injuries – in the shock of the crash, you may not have noticed them. Once you're away from the plane, sit down and wait for rescuers.

TOP TIP! You'll be more likely to survive a crash if you plan an escape when you board. Count the seats between you and the exit, so you can feel your way in the dark.

ACKNOWLEDGMENTS

Pages: 1 Photodisc; 2–3 Yellowstone National Park, Corbis/Tim Davis; 4–5 Corbis/Meijert de Haan/EPA; 6–7 Corbis/Fabrice Coffrini; 8–9 Corbis/Michael S. Yamashita; 10–11 Photodisc; 12 Lyn Topinka/USGS, inset Corbis/Bettmann Archives; 13 Rex/Sipa Press; 14 FLPA; 16 Corbis/TWPhoto; 17 Reuters/Stringer; 18tl David Rydevik; 18tr Nature/Photodisc;18br Corbis/Ashley Cooper; 19tr Science Photo Library/David A Hardry/Futures; 20 BBC Photo Library, London; 21 Corbis/Ralph A. Clevenger; 21b Corbis/Lake County Museum; 22 Corbis/Michael Hanschke/dpa; 23t Corbis/Mike Theiss/Ultimate Chase; 23b Corbis/Reuters; 24t Rex Features/RS/Keystone USA; 24b Corbis/Bettmann Archives; 25 Rex Features; 26 Corbis/Thierry Orban; 27 Corbis/ Layne Kennedy; 28 Yellowstone National Park; 29 Corbis/Simela Pantzartzi/EPA; 30 Corbis/Tony Arruza; 31 Corbis/Jim Zuckerman; 32 Getty Images/Martin Baumann/AFP; 33 Corbis/Larry W. Smith/EPA; 34 Corbis/Eric Nguyen; 35 Corbis; 35 Corbis/ Chris Collins; 36 Corbis/Michael Freeman; 37 Corbis/Andrew Brown/Ecoscene; 38 Corbis/ Carol Hughes/Gallo Images; 39t Corbis/Meijert de Haan/EPA; 39b Corbis/Chris Hellier; 40 Corbis/Scott Stulberg; 41 Nebojsa Kovacevic; 42 Corbis/Jenifer Brown/Star Ledger; 43 Corbis/ Karen Kasmauski; 45 Corbis; 46 Corbis/Galen Rowell; 47 Corbis/Jerome Minet/Kipa; 48 Corbis/Ashley Cooper; 49t Corbis/Uli Wiesmeier, 49b Corbis/Charlie Munsey; 50 Corbis/SYGMA; 51 Corbis/Tobias Bernhard/Zefa/Corbis; 52 Kaj Sorensen; 53 Corbis/Momatiuk–Eastcott; 54 Nature/Pete Oxford; 55 Corbis/John Van Hasselt; 58t Corbis/Peter Johnson; 58b Corbis/Ryan Pyle; 59 Nature/Photodisc; 60t Corbis/Darren Staples/Reuters; 60b Corbis/Karen Kasmauski; 61t Corbis/Christopher Morris; 61b Nature/Photodisc; 62 Corbis/Tom Bean; 63 Corbis/Galen Rowell; 64 Corbis/Kevin Schafer; 65 Corbis/John Carnemolla; 67b Corbis/Joe McDonald; 68 Corbis/Martin Harvey; 69 Corbis/Martin Harvey; 70t Photodisc; 71 Corbis/Theo Allofs; 72t Corbis/Gary W. Carter; 72b Corbis/Joe McDonald; 73 Corbis/Buddy Mays; 74t Rex Features/Karen Paolillo; 74b Corbis/Arthur Morris; 75t Rex Features/Sipa Press; 76 Rex Features/DPPI; 77 Corbis/Tim Davis; 78 Rex Features/James D. Morgan; 79 FLPA/David Hosking; 80t Photodisc; 80b Yellowstone National Park; 81t Corbis/Renee Lynn; 82 Photodisc; 83 Photodisc; 84 Corbis/Frank Lukasseck; 85 Rex Features/Nature Picture Library; 86 Corbis/Lothar Lenz; 87 Rex Features/Patrick Frilet; 89 Corbis/Kevin Schafer; 90 Rex Features/Nature Picture Library; 91 Rex Features/CDC/Phanie; 93t Science Photo Library/Peter Scoones; 93b Corbis /Reuters; 94 Rex/Jo Mahy/Splashdown Direct; 95 Rex Features/Nature Picture Library; 96 Rex Features/Nature Picture Library; 97 Corbis/ Jeffrey L. Rotman; 98–99 Corbis/Zefa/Markus Moellenberg; 100 Corbis/Bettmann; 101 Rex Features; 102 Rex Features/Ken McKay/Andrew Murray; 103 NPS photo/Harlan Kredit; 104t Rex Features/DPPI; 105t Corbis/Paul A. Souders; 105b Getty Images/AFP/Johannes Simon; 106 Corbis/Bill Stormont; 107 Corbis/Alejandro Ernesto; 108 Rex Features/Bob Bowen; 109 Photodisc; 110 Rex Features/Sipa Press; 111 Rex Features/Keystone

Illustrations

Pages: 15 Gill Tomblin/Simon Gurr; 19b Nick Tibbott; 27b Cecilia Bandiera; 44 Gill Tomblin/Simon Gurr; 53b Nick Tibbott; 56-57 Gill Tomblin/Simon Gurr; 64 Joanne Cowne; 66t Alan Male; 66b Gill Tomblin/Simon Gurr; 67a Alan Male; 70b Gill Tomblin/Simon Gurr; 75 Gill Tomblin/Nick Tibbott; 81 Nick Tibbott; 88 Alan Male; 92 Gill Tomblin/Nick Tibbott; 95 Alan Male; 104b Simon Gurr

CONTENTS

Introduction

Welcome to retirement! Congratulations on making it over the all the hurdles and reaching that wonderful time of life where you get to do whatever you want. No more morning commute, no more idiotic bosses, no more stressful deadlines! You are now officially off the clock and the world is your oyster! While it may seem easy to just settle back and continue doing the things we have always done, why not mix it up a bit, break the inertia and get out and try something new? What have you got to lose?

There is no need to be bound by convention, push the envelope, do it weird, do it different, but most of all do it fun! Be that cigar chomping rock'n'roll granny if it takes your fancy. Seriously, if your kids aren't worried about what you are up to, then you are probably not doing it right!

When I set out to write this book my aim was to crack open the unexplored world and have a look at what there is out there. It was never my intention to give excessively detailed instructions on any given suggestion, (and I think I have pretty well succeeded on that count), nor was it my intention to offer a load of patronizing advice on how to manage your finances, eat healthily or stay fit. (I am fairly certain that no one wants or needs my opinion on how they aught to manage their life). That said, there is an exciting world of possibilities out there that very few of us get the chance to explore during our working lives, but retirement is that time! The following pages contain far more than the promised 101 suggestions, so if you find some of them a bit lame or not quite to your taste feel free to view them as a unwanted bonus gifts (not unlike those free steak knifes that come with every product ever sold on TV), and enjoy the rest.

On a personal note: Before you start reading I have a bit of a confession to make. When I sat down to write this book I had every intention of writing a totally 'straight' book with nothing too weird or wacky in it, but as is often the way with me things pretty soon ran off the rails. In spite of my best efforts to keep my quirky in check it kept leaking out onto the page. In the end I decided to just go with it and I added the subtitle. As a result what initially began as a fairly normal book gets intermittently weirder as it goes along. While it starts out in a reasonably conventional fashion it soon starts to get a bit strange. I pulled it all back into line several times and of course, me being me, it just kept getting weird again. At first this bothered me, I had no idea how I was going to finish the book if I tried to take all my peculiarities out, but once I freed myself from the shackles of expectation I began to really enjoy the mix of the two, so I decided to leave it that way. I hope the mix works you too. After all, retirement is all about having the freedom to do it the way you want to, so I did. I sincerely hope you enjoy!

What Is Retirement?

English is a notoriously difficult language. As the bastard son of the Latin, Nordic and Teutonic language groups, it has so many homonyms and synonyms that trying to accurately define the meaning of anything can be enough to make your brain bleed. Given English's linguistic latitude it should come as no surprise that the word 'retirement' has many variations in meaning, each with its own shades, colours and overtones, and that any definition is going to be subject to interpretation. So, when seeking to understand what is meant by retirement, the first stop is quite naturally the dictionary.

What Is Retirement

www.dictionary.com describes retirement thus:

1.The act of retiring, withdrawing, or leaving; the state of being retired.

2.The act of retiring or of leaving one's job, career, or occupation permanently, usually because of age: *"I'm looking forward to my retirement from teaching"*.

3.The portion of a person's life during which a person is retired: *"What will you do in retirement?"*

4. Removal of something from service or use: *Retirement of the space shuttle fleet.*

5.Withdrawal of a jury from a courtroom to deliberate in private on a verdict.

6.Orderly withdrawal of a military force, according to plan, without pressure from the enemy.

Personally, I am not at all satisfied with these definitions. With the best will in the world they have failed to capture the dramatic and exciting nature of the occasion! All this 'leaving' and 'withdrawing' is pretty damn dour; and choosing to frame one's retirement in such terms could be a tad depressing. So, in the joyous spirit of reinvention I would like to propose a bit of a rewrite.

1.The act of retiring, withdrawing, or leaving; the state of being retired.

Really, this definition is quite awful, and totally backward looking! The fact is you cannot 'withdraw from' or 'leave' one place without moving to another, so why put all the focus on the leaving? Why not put a little more emphasis on where you are going? It could just as easily read something like this:

1.The act of retiring, entering a new self-determined phase of life, leaving the employ or oversight of others to exercise greater choice and freedom in the use of one's time; the state of being retired.

How much better is that? Who wouldn't want to "exercise greater choice and freedom in the use of ones time"? It's like a lottery win.

2.The act of retiring or of leaving one's job, career, or occupation permanently, usually because of age: *"I'm looking forward to my retirement from teaching."*

This one is troublesome in a number of ways, as it suggests that one is leaving one's "career or occupation permanently". Naturally if one is leaving a job they hate then popping the cork on the bubbly is entirely appropriate; but if you have a career or occupation that you love, one might not feel so inclined to celebrate, particularly if the choice to retire was not entirely your own. However, all is not lost. In almost every field imaginable there are options to continue your beloved life's work in some form or another. Teachers can become private tutors and mentors. Hairdressers can have clients call by the house. Stockbrokers can still trade on the Internet. Many retired builders give great service in hardware stores. Your lifetime of skills and knowledge is of great value and there is absolutely no reason to set it aside if you don't want to. This definition could just as rightly read:

2.The act of retiring, to permanently leave one's job, career, or occupation: or to reduce or restructure one's level of workplace involvement to better suit one's changing desires and capacities, after many years of work: *"I'm looking forward to my retirement from teaching, and taking up part time tutoring".*

After all retirement doesn't mean stopping dead in ones tracks, (unless of course you want to).

OK, this next one is dead easy.

3. The portion of a person's life during which a person is retired: *"What will you do in retirement?"*
Becomes:

3. The portion of a person's life during which one's activity is totally self-determined, and one is no longer required to work for a living: *"What will you do in retirement?"*

A much happier option I think!

---

4. Removal of something from service or use: *Retirement of the space shuttle fleet.*

This is more or less OK as it is, although in this context the word removal has a bit of a harsh overtone. It would seem like much more fun if it read:

4. Removing the burden of 'service or use" imposed on a person or object by forces beyond their control. *Retirement of the space shuttle fleet.* (At last the poor thing can finally relax, all that launching and re-entering can really take a toll).

5.Withdrawal of a jury from a courtroom to deliberate in private on a verdict.

This one I actually like, as it is one of the few definitions that is proactive. That jury is off to do something important. They are going to apply their minds, utilise their critical faculties and exercise moral judgement. This is the kind of retirement that I can relate to!

6.Orderly withdrawal of a military force, according to plan, without pressure from the enemy.

This is probably the best definition of the lot. What could be better than the ceasing of hostilities and the withdrawal of troops? Imagine a world where we could retire all the armies, now that would really be something.

OK, now that we have some more upbeat interpretations of what retirement actually is, it's time to give some thought as to how you would like to define your retirement.

Sea Change Or Tree Change?

I'm going to keep this short. Are you in the right place? Do you need to move somewhere more suitable to your interests, physical needs or budget? If so, this is the first thing you should attend to. If you are going to create a new life for yourself then you need to get the foundation right. No point in investing vast amounts of energy building a network of new friends and location specific activities if you are going to up stumps and move in six months. Carpe Diem, I say! If you are going to do the change, best get on with it!

What About The Finances?

No one needs a lot of money. Having lived most my life as a freelancer working in the arts, I can say this with a good deal of authority! Creativity, curiosity, kindness and a sense of adventure will make you happier and bring you more genuine friends than any amount of money in the bank. If you have money, that's great. However, if you don't have much money then life has issued you a challenge, but it is a challenge you can meet! Most creative endeavours don't require a lot of cash. If your financial circumstances dictate that you must choose from inexpensive options just remember, your imagination has no such limitations. Your novel can be just as epic as the novel written by a millionaire! Your picnic can be just as wonderful as a dinner at a celebrity-studded restaurant. Think outside the box, you will be amazed at all the possibilities lurking out there!

What Kind Of Retirement?

No matter what age we are, there are certain things that everyone requires in order to feel happy and fulfilled. We all need the friendship, love and companionship of like-minded people. We all need healthy food, fresh air and clean water. We all need time to ourselves to reflect. We all need to challenge ourselves and push our boundaries, and last, but by no means least, we all need a sense of purpose. Unfortunately for many people, one or more of these things often falls by the wayside when we are mired in the daily grind of work, mortgage and small children. All too often life rushes by and somehow we end up at the end of our working lives feeling like we have missed our calling. Fortunately we now live in an age where most of us can expect two, three, maybe even four decades of reasonably good health in retirement, in which we can live true to our own sense of purpose. For some people retirement can span well over half their adult life, so the last thing you'd want to do is waste it! Human life is so precious, and having been granted such a gift there really is no excuse for not getting out there and doing whatever it is that makes you happy!

No matter what your finances, inclinations or capacity, the world is overflowing with possibilities. Not only have we been blessed with extraordinary minds, we have been given dexterous hands (with opposable thumbs), complex language, and a strong desire to better ourselves. Whatever else we may be, we humans are fundamentally goal oriented, achievement driven beings that thrive on challenge and purpose, and that doesn't change just because we hit retirement.

So, now that you are free to go wherever and do whatever you like, what is it that you actually want to do? How on earth do you choose? There are so many incredible options it can be difficult to narrow it down. Most of us have an inclination towards particular interests and activities, but few of us have explored all the possibilities available within those spheres. If, for example, you have dreamed of spending your retirement cruising the Bahamas on your hundred-foot yacht but your finances don't look like they will stretch that far, do not despair. If you think laterally you may find your favourite activities can be done on a shoestring; or you can devise a plan B from the extraordinary range of activities that cost little or no money at all. Whatever your dreams you don't need millions. The world is stuffed stupid with fun and rewarding things to do and you now have the luxury of time and choice.

Of course, what ever you do you will need to prioritize. Anything that requires robust health, like that trek up Everest, is probably something you should do sooner rather than later, whereas reading the complete works of Dostoevsky could possibly wait a bit. But what ever your health, budget or life circumstances, there is a full and wonderful life to be lived. There are flavours to taste, flowers to smell, songs to be sung and boundless joy to be had. Your life is now 100% YOURS, and it is really only just beginning! You now have the reigns firmly in your hands, so get out there and live it LARGE!

To make this book easier to navigate I have sorted it into the broad categories of arty, crafty, literary, political, social, educational, hedonistic, the great outdoors, performing, voyeuristic, charitable, family oriented, nomadic, musical, sporty, spiritual, technical and the life aquatic. I suggest you read them all though, as you may find quite a number of things that pique your interest listed in sections that you would have never previously considered.

WARNING!

This book is not entirely factually accurate. It contains some thoroughly bad advice and may cause injury or death if taken too seriously. Some of the activities described herein may be fun to talk about but are decidedly unfun to do! Proceed with caution, you have been warned!

ARTISTIC

Many people have dreamed of living an artistic life, only to find the practical demands of the world have proved too great an obstacle. When one is working full time there can be little energy left at the end of the day for artistic endeavours, but now you have your freedom you can let your artistic side run wild. You may unleash a powerfully weird talent that has been lurking deep inside just waiting for its chance to emerge. Whether you are tossing aside convention and conjuring up abstract images of pure imagination, or interpreting a carefully staged still life, creating something from nothing is one of this world's most satisfying experiences. There is boundless joy, beauty and freedom to be found in the visual arts.

Arts and crafts can be amazingly social too; there are all kinds of groups, classes, and societies where people share tips and tricks, and bitch about each other's work. There are even groups that get together to contribute to larger works. Kids also love getting messy with arts and crafts, so what better way to engage your grand-kids than to get their best clothes covered in paint and glitter before you send them back home?

Picture This

Whether you choose to paint, draw, sketch or print, in our post-modern world NO RULES apply! You can throw paint, scratch, scrawl, drip, smear, daub, do what ever takes your fancy. There are literally thousands of online courses, groups and classes you can explore. Most cities have a favourite spot where artists tend to gather on sunny a day, so why not dig out your easel and get out there and join them. There are also countless opportunities to exhibit your work; from galleries to local coffee shops, everyone wants art! If a picture paints a thousand words, why not have your say?

Painting

Personally I love throwing paint around. I put everything into my abstracts; old train or theatre tickets, coins, newspaper, I even use cheap acrylic gap filler for an impasto medium. (Impasto is a thick textured layer in an artwork). There's no need to go to the expense of investing in professional paints. If you are simply a pleasure-seeking dabbler on a budget you could try creating with watercolours, aquarelles (watercolour pencil) or acrylic paints. You can get going for next to nothing. The old house paint stashed in the garage will do just fine to start with. Local discount stores are awash with inexpensive art supplies that are perfectly fine. I used our old sample pots with a kid's brush sets and cheap dime store canvasses to make stunning artworks for my house. I even sold a few paintings!

But really you don't even need paper or canvases; you can paint on an old sheet, a piece of Masonite, or even a cardboard box. Of course if you are drawn to something a bit more refined you can always build up a collection of quality art materials over time, but it's certainly not necessary to get you started. All you need is imagination and bravery and you are on your way.

Drawing

Why not check out a life drawing class. You don't need pricey brushes or expensive paints, all you need is a piece of charcoal and you are up and running. If you are on a tight budget then drawing with pencils, or even cartooning with felt pens and coloured ink, are delightfully inexpensive ways of getting an image onto paper. However, if you fancy your self as a potential Picasso (and you're not afraid of the cost), you might even want to try some of the more expensive forms such as quality coloured pencils, Conte crayons or soft pastels.

Printmaking

Printmaking has been steadily growing in popularity ever since Gutenberg pulled the first print off his revolutionary press. Of course, printing a book or magazine is not the same as making art, but the fundamental principals have been well adapted to the cause. Whether you choose one of the more demanding "high art" methods, such as screen-printing or lithograph, or one of your kitchen table varieties like potato or linoleum cut, printmaking is a truly beautiful art form. If you don't have a lot of cash to splash you could simply get together with the grand-kids and stamp cheap acrylic paints onto calico or butcher's paper with hand carved potato cuts. But if you want to go a bit more high end there plenty of classes and studios out there where you can learn to etch copper plates or make silk screens, and more importantly get your hands on the necessary equipment.

Collage

Cut out, juxtapose and stick down, these are the three commandments of collage. As an art form, collage is especially good for social commentary. Many contemporary news and science magazines make great fodder for keen the social commentator. Collage has also moved into the digital age. This is most clearly on display in the proliferation of online memes. In fact, some creative type is probably busy right now cutting and pasting Donald Trump's head onto the body of a chicken, and emblazoning it with some pithy remark. You can, of course, just get decorative with the form, but there are so many outrageous images out there, both printed and digital; it's hard to resist the temptation to get a little bit political.

Become An Art Critic

While technically not art in itself, becoming and art critic is a great way to get involved in the arts without having to have any special artistic skills or talents. After all, art is all about the attitude and the expression. In the art word the execution of an idea is never as important as impressing random cravat wearing people with your inscrutable, multi-syllabic art-speak. Playing art critic is loads of fun. Most people will be completely baffled by what you are saying, but will still stroke their chins thoughtfully, nod in agreement and throw back another red wine.

However, if you are having a bit of trouble coming up with the necessary inane art-speak to make your commentary seem deep and important enough, don't worry. As always the Internet has the solution. Introducing the "arty bollocks generator".

http://www.artybollocks.com/

The arty bollocks generator invites you to "Generate your own artist statement for free, and if you don't like it, generate another one. Feel free to use the statements with funding applications, exhibitions, curriculum vitae, websites etc."

Example: *"This work comments on the deconstruction of structuralism. It's about humanity's existential struggle for a segregated autonomy within in the post isolationist miasma that is an inherent feature of life within the critical density of mass urban colonization"* Instant critic! How good is that?

Get Into "Street Art"

Depending on where you live, street art is either considered graffiti or a revered art form that enhances amenity and social inclusion. But whatever it is, it is not just for teenagers. Many cities have places where street art is encouraged. If you are lucky enough to live in one of those places, why not get out there and make your mark. If not talk to the local authorities and see if you can get a designated "art space" going. When done in a properly allocated space, street art provides a fantastic forum for cross-generational communication and community engagement. As a case in point, in a city near me the local authority turned over an abandoned factory to street artists, and it now draws huge crowds of tourists every weekend.

Snap Into Photography

Whether it is a candid snap or staged masterpiece, photography is an art form. With the click of button a photograph distils the essence of a moment, reflecting the deeper truths of our existence. A photograph can shift perceptions, alter our constructs of reality and reveal untold stories that have the power to profoundly change our lives. *(See that arty bollocks really does come in handy).*

All bollocks aside, you don't need to have a top-notch kit to catch a moment in your lens. If you have a half way decent camera on your phone it's more than good enough to start with; and there are a huge range of stunning filters and effects available on apps like Instagram and Hipstermatic that you can download to your phone for free. There is also an ever-growing collection of inexpensive lenses for under $50 that you can clip onto your smart phone camera for a more professional result. If budget is a concern then using your smart phone to shoot spontaneous, un-staged subject matter, (such as urban photography or nature photography) is an excellent way to go.

However, if you would prefer to get your self a decent SLR camera it's good to know they have never been more affordable. And of course, digital photography means no more film or processing, so once you have the camera you can keep on shooting with no additional outlay.

If you are reasonably computer savvy there are wonderful photo editing programs like GIMP that are available for free (and loads of YouTube tutorials available to teach you how to use them), so you don't have to outlay thousands to use top notch programs like Adobe Photoshop, (although you can now subscribe to adobe's complete range of drawing, layout and photo editing software for a small monthly fee, so it could be worth signing up for a month or two to see if it is for you).

Once you have a portfolio of works you could mount an exhibition. There are plenty of inexpensive, good looking, "art" frames available at places like IKEA and you can get high quality prints done at your local print centre. Alternately, you could start an online gallery, set up a web site, or offer your shots for download on a "stock image" site*. There are also lot's of places like "www.shutterfly.com" where you can have your shots printed on a canvas, T-shirt or coffee mug, or assembled into a high quality printed book or calendar. What better way to make personalised gifts for your family and friends?

*(Offering your photos for sale on stock image sites can bring in a fair bit of cash if your shots prove to be popular. I recommend you try "www.bigstock.com" It's a popular choice for amateur and professional photographers alike.)

Sculpt Another Reality

With extraordinary works like Salvador Dali's giant poo covered building to Jeff Comb's "puppy", sculpture is now officially out of the box. You can make practically anything. Make a moo fish, a winged cat or a gigantic eyeball on a stick. No matter what the medium, the limit is your imagination. You don't have to do expensive bronze cast statues or chisel marble like Michelangelo; all kinds of everyday household junk can be turned into sculptural masterpieces. Clay, papier- mâché, chicken wire, plaster of Paris, old toilet roll centres, railway sleepers, used drink bottles, wax, cd's, dead bicycles, old TVs, rusting farm equipment, anything can be turned into a sculpture.

I am currently building a sculptural "Birth of the robot Venus/Medusa" out of an old clam shaped toddler pool, a mannequin and some old ipads, TV's, cell phones and bag of old toy snakes for the hair. *(Although to be honest, I'm not at all sure what I am going to do with it, once it's finished).*

I admit there are some sculptural some forms, like welding or fibreglass, that require a fair bit of cash and an excess of shed space, but there are plenty of smaller projects that are inexpensive, not quite so space hungry and relatively easy to do. For example, carving aerated concrete blocks is particularly good for making garden sculptures. Aerated concrete is readily available in a range of sizes at most building suppliers. It is remarkably inexpensive, lightweight and can even be chiselled with a butter knife. What's more, it looks totally stunning, it's extremely easy to work with and you can achieve some very impressive results without too much practice or skill. With aerated concrete you could turn your garden into a miniature sculpture park with very little effort.

If you need a little more inspiration try Googling up images of "Sculpture by the sea" (which is the world's largest annual sculpture exhibition), and check out some of the amazing works.

Become An Artists Model

If you like the fine arts and enjoy the company of artists, but really don't feel like creating your own; why not get a gig as an artist's model? If the idea of being paid to sit around with your kit off floats your boat then this one is definitely for you. It's one of the very few activities you can do naked where the older (and less conventionally perfect) your body is, the more they love you. Bumps, rolls, cellulite and pot-bellies; artists just adore them. After all, the more unique your body, the more interesting and challenging you are to draw. The money isn't bad either!

CRAFTY

If the idea of doing "high art" doesn't appeal you might fancy directing your creative drive into something a little more practical. For centuries artisans have used their imagination, their sense of design and their manual skills to make all kinds of beautiful, practical things that serve humanity.

Pottery

Slick and slippery, oozing ones fingers through slimy clay on a potters wheel is pure magic. Hand-crafted pottery pieces are not only unique; they can also be extremely useful. Stunning hand painted plates, platters and bowls grace many of the finest tables.

Potters clay is inexpensive and easily obtained from your local arts supply. If you do not have a potter's wheel or a kiln there are lots studios and classes where you can try your hand; or you could simply start with a lump of clay and try hand shaping the object of your desire. For those that don't have access to a kiln there are "self-hardening" or "air dried" clays available on the market; I even heard of someone baking their clay in the microwave. As for the glazing side of things, as long as it is not being used for the dining table you can simply paint and seal your creation with regular house paint and a good strong polyurethane. There are also a number of different coloured modelling clays, such as "Fimo" or "Das" available that you can bake in the oven to harden. These products are wonderful for finer work like jewellery making. From pendants, earrings and bracelets to fruit bowls and garden pots, there is no limit to what you can make.

Sew What?

You will be relieved to know that the days of making lace tissue box covers are officially over. Today you can design and make absolutely anything, and the wilder the better! Make yourself a hat, a coat, a dress, or a pair of rabbit ears. You could make fancy dress costumes for Halloween, or an Edwardian gown for a cross dresser.

If you are not up for designing something from scratch many charity shops have boxes full of old paper patterns that you can adapt to suit your imagination. My mother regularly scours the charity shops for old curtains and fabrics to sew up into wild and strange garments. She even started a fashion label called Wonky Wear and sells her creations on consignment at a number of wacky "alternative" emporiums.

Create kooky gifts for your relatives, or make yourself a belly dancing costume. The world is overflowing with hideous old wedding and bridesmaid dresses. If you use your imagination they can be a rich source of amazing fabrics to chop, splice, hack, recycle and reconstruct into all kinds of fun and outrageous outfits. A one off prom dress for a relative that wants to stand out, a wench's outfit for your next trip to medieval world, or a pirate costume for your spouse. Anything really!

Model Making

If sculpture seems a bit too overwhelming, but you still like the idea of making something three dimensional, model making could be just the thing. Unlike sculptures, which are usually either an artist's abstract creation, or the more conventional 3D likeness of a person, model making is simply the art of creating miniature versions of real things, such as trains, cars or aeroplanes.

While not exactly considered a "high art", model making does require a great deal of skill and patience, particularly if you are designing and creating your own models from scratch. Architects, for example, make the most extraordinary models to bring their visions into 3d form for their clients. However, if you are not into designing you own models, but are more of a specialist in a particular type of car/train/plane or motorbike, there are literally thousands of different model kits available to cater to all tastes and budgets.

Knit With Wit

The artless pastel baby booties and matinee jackets of the past are long gone. Knitting and crocheting have making a bit of comeback in recent times and it no longer means abandoning your wild side. Knitting is now a full on artistic endeavour! All kinds of people are clamouring for beautifully designed original works, and not just in wool. Raffia, slub cotton, spun hemp, mohair, alpaca, jute; all kinds of natural fibres are finding a place in the creative knitter's basket. Knitting needn't be expensive either. You can recycle old jumpers from the thrift store. There are some amazing quality wools lurking in hideous old jumpers that are so out of date that no one in right mind would wear them out in public. You can pick them up for a song and unravel them ready for re-purposing. Why not make

something totally outrageous. Here's a challenge, see if you can out-viral the knitting artist Anna Maltz's famous nude suits? (Seriously, you should Google knitted nude suit, and check them out... they are extraordinary!)

Leather-work

Leather-work spans a wide range of aesthetics, from hippy to punk, to high-end designer wear, it offers something for just about everyone, (except of course your die hard vegan). Purses, bags, clothing, wallets, belts, jewellery, shoes, bottle holders, key rings, art works and certain unmentionable "indoor recreational outfits" for British MPs; there are so many things you can make with leather. The tools needed are minimal and relatively inexpensive. All you need is a sharp knife, a hole punch, needles or a sewing machine, sculpting tools and a hammer (for making artistic impressions), buckles and studs as required, and glue.

Make An American Quilt

Whether you get together with friends for a ritual stitch and bitch, or sit quietly quilting, there is no limit to the possibilities for this traditional American art form. There is a vast network of quilters out there, with regular conventions and exhibitions; they even have dedicated websites and chat rooms. Quilters are known for getting together to swap patterns and fabric swatches, and many groups meet up regularly to work on large collective projects.

While making an American quilt is traditionally a quiet and refined activity, it doesn't have to be. There is absolutely no need to stick with the traditional forms. For example Gothic quilting artist Ben Venom is making some truly original pieces that are taking this time-honoured craft into totally uncharted territory. Why not subvert the quilting conventions yourself and make something totally outrageous. Let your imagination run wild. Express your inner world in appliqué!

Bear Quilt by Ben Venom

Jewellery Making

Jewellery can be so much more than just a choking hazard for the grand-kids. It can be a wonderfully unique way to express your self. Whether you go wild with beads, channelling your inner Masai, or drape yourself with gold, silver and diamonds, jewellery is totally fabulous.

It's true, some jewellery making may require extreme heat or hammering, but you can make jewellery out of just about anything. Coloured glass, painted beads, wire, aluminium flashing, epoxy resins, safety pins, buttons, papier-mâché, practically anything can be turned into a body adornment. Pull apart old necklaces and restring them into stunning earrings, beading is dead easy. Make mad pendants. Drape yourself in colour, go nuts! Your young relatives might love to receive a necklace or bracelet that you have made especially for them.

Whittling

Whittling is believed to have been with us since the Middle to Upper Palaeolithic period, when it was the main source of spears and hunting arrows that allowed our ancient ancestors to thrive and survive.

It is also one of the cheapest and most readily accessible crafts around. All you need is a sharp knife and a chunk of wood. "The Art of Manliness" describes whittling as *"a great pastime for the man who wants to craft something, but may not have the room or tools to build a dining room table"*, but this doesn't mean that whittling is just for men. I have a female friend who has created the most extraordinary collection of hand-whittled spoons. She loves the meditative peace and calm of simply working with wood.

Hand Whittled Spoons by Kate Smiley

Softwoods are the best for beginners because they are considerably easier to cut and shape, whereas hard-woods require a little more patience and skill. Woods with a straight grain tend to give a better result, (as they are considerably easier to work with than woods that have the grain going in multiple directions). Avoid woods with lots of knots, as the knots can cause unwanted irregularities, weaken or even break your work.

Lumber yards, craft stores and woodlands where it is permitted to gather fallen branches are all great places to gather supplies. Popular whittling woods are:

BASS WOOD: A soft wood without much grain, basswood has been used by carvers for centuries. In fact German sculptors used to use it for crafting stunning Gothic altarpieces in the middle ages. You can pick up blocks of basswood in most good craft stores, and it's not usually too expensive.

PINE: While a traditional whittling wood, pine has its pluses and minuses. On the plus side it is soft, easy to cut and readily available. On the down side some people feel it doesn't hold detail all that well; and if you are using fresh pine it can be quite sappy, which can leave your fingers and knife quite sticky.

BALSA WOOD: Most of us have some memory of using balsa wood as children. It is one of the mainstays of many crafts, including model making. Balsa is extremely soft, remarkably inexpensive and incredibly flexible. You can use it to make just about anything.

FOUND TWIGS AND BRANCHES: Many people mistakenly believe that you need to buy wood to whittle. This is manifestly not true. Found twigs and branches (from just about any kind of tree) are perfectly suitable for whittling. Sure your creation may be a bit more rustic when you are using random bits of wood but that is all part of the charm.

You don't need a special whittling knife (although they are available). A sharp pocketknife is good enough to get you started.

WARNING: Even though this goes without saying I am going to say it anyway: When working with sharp knives you need be careful. No one wants to find you covered in blood looking like you just went ten rounds with an axe murderer. Don't rush, take your time, and if you are new to the task take some precautions. A pair of good solid work gloves could go a long way to keeping all your fingers firmly attached to your hands.

Felting

No one is sure whether this ancient eastern craft was first developed in the Middle East or the Far East, but wherever it may have come from no one disputes the fact that FELTING is an age-old practice. Over the centuries felting has evolved into several unique styles, each originating from a different tribe and/or place.

Today felting is practiced by all kinds of people, from nomads on the great plains of Asia (who are still living in traditional felt yurts), to kids in the

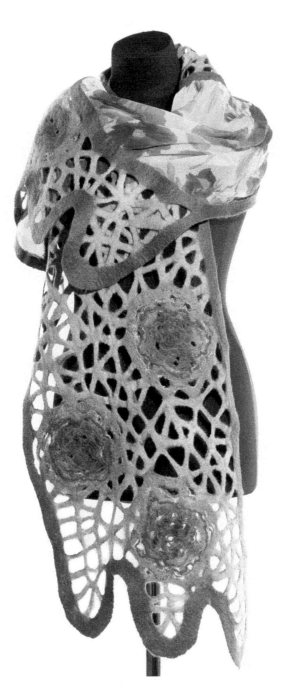

Hand Felted Scarf

local kindergarten. There are several simple felting techniques that don't require much in the way of experience or tools, and given the rough and imperfect nature of the form any "mistakes" simply add to the texture and interest of the work.

WET FELTING or FELT MAKING: is the practice of using soap and water on a fibre (most commonly sheep's wool) to make a felted fabric. There is no spinning, knitting, crocheting or weaving involved.

FULLING or KNIT FELTING: is the practice of taking a knitted, crocheted or woven garment and then shrinking it to fill the holes between the stitches. The technique of "fulling" is often used to great effect by those making highly original hats, scarves and wraps.

NEEDLE FELTING: doesn't require soap and water and does not necessarily need to be done with an animal fibre. Needle felting is done by using "felting needles" to apply additional fibres to enhance a fabric or garment (those can be made of felted material or knitted, crocheted or woven material), You can even use it make decorative figurines.

ART FELT is similar to needle felting but, instead of adding fibres to an existing garment you add your fibres onto a special backing paper that dissolves in water. Once you have finished adding your fibres you simply wash your work. The backing paper will dissolve leaving you with just the finished product.

No matter which style or tradition takes your fancy felting is the perfect art form for anyone who likes earthy, natural, random shapes and textures. If you have had enough of straight lines this could well be for you. Felting supplies are readily available on EBay, at your local craft store or in your local shearing shed.

Scrap-booking

Mythologise your family's history by setting out your photos, awards and show tickets in luxurious books filled with pretty coloured cardboard and decorative paper. This is seriously good fun, and takes up much less space in the living room than that overflowing trophy cabinet. You don't have to stop at using photographs and other paper items either. If you want to make your scrapbook a bit more voodoo friendly you could always include things like first-teeth and locks of hair.

Candle Making

Hot wax is good for so much more than just yanking out unwanted body hair. Whether you want to make gifts for the relatives, sell your creations, set the stage for some serious "low-light" romance, or get a lot of burly young firemen to come over, candle making can accommodate. There are so many shapes, colours and scents you can use to create a something that is totally unique to you. Candle making is truly an art form in its own right.

Soap Making

If you are having problems with an under-washed person in your life, handing them a gift of handmade soap, while telling them you would like them to use it and let you know what they think, could be the perfect way to drop them a helpful hint. (It's so much subtler than just shoving a bar of Dove into their hand).

But seriously, soap making is a wonderful way to make original artisan gifts, and it could save you a small fortune come Christmas. This simple, time honoured process can be done with common household ingredients, such as olive oil, coconut oil, Shea butter, goat or sheep's milk, lye, essential oils, flower petals and oatmeal etc. The Internet has countless recipes that you can either follow directly, or use as a base to make your own personal varieties.

WARNING: Be extremely careful when using lye (AKA: Caustic Soda). It is can cause serious burns in its concentrated form. The first time I made soap I accidentally let a flake of lye fall onto the kitchen bench. When I wiped down the bench to make a sandwich the lye dissolved and ended up being absorbed into the bread. One bite was enough to burn a small welt on my lip. I recommend rubber gloves and putting newspaper down on all surfaces.

Spinning And Weaving

For thousands of years spinning and weaving were the methods we used to make textiles to clothe ourselves. Before spinning and weaving we had to wear animal skins to keep us warm, which was all a bit smelly and draughty. Of course, once we worked out how to make yarns and fabrics our clothing options expanded exponentially. Like so many other artisan crafts, the making of hand-hewn yarns and fabrics is now considered a bespoke art form in its own right. Whether you are spinning up some lumpy alpaca yarn for a scarf or weaving up an intricate tapestry or tartan, spinning and weaving are joyous, meditative, creative pastimes. They are not too taxing on the body. They don't require flaming heat or dangerous chemicals, and the equipment is not prohibitively expensive. You can buy a spinning wheel on EBay for anything from $100 to $1000 dollars and you can pick up a loom from as little as $5 for a kid's craft model. While a serious loom can cost over a $1000, you should be able to pick up a decent starter loom for less than $150.

Decoupage

For the uninitiated decoupage is the art of decorating three-dimensional objects with images. (At last, a use for all those expired coupons and old copies of National Geographic). Collage is a genuine art form, and can include so much more than just printed images. Found objects, old coins, seed pods, pressed leaves, absolutely anything. There is no limit to the social commentary you can make with some old magazines and a glue stick. You could do an art piece that comments on disposable consumer culture by covering some Ikea furniture with decoupage cuts outs from an Ikea catalogue. (And yes, while that may be a random, pointless suggestion, it would definitely be a talking point).

HEAD TO YOUR SHED

Man caves, she sheds, everyone loves somewhere they can go and do their own thing. Whether you want to indulge in some creative mechanics, set up a pottery kiln or simply read a book and revel in your solitude, your shed is your haven. It's that magical place where you can do all those messy, filthy, space hungry things that your spouse won't let you do inside the house. A list that includes, but is by no means limited to the following suggestions:

Blacksmithing

Did you know that going back 150 years roughly 20% of census respondents listed their occupation as blacksmith? It's not really that surprising when you think about all the armour, horse shoes, swords, shields, door furniture, hooks, gates, fence posts, plant stands, wheels, barrel strapping, candelabras, hinges, locks and red hot pokers etc., that were forged in personal foundries. However with hand forged items selling at a huge premium these days, people tend to view ironwork as an artisan hobby, (although clearly not one for the feint hearted).

If you are going to take up smiting you are going to need pumping muscles, a strong back, a large well ventilated space, a forge or furnace that can pump out heat of up to 1400 degrees Fahrenheit, (most likely a coal or propane, but propane is much cleaner), some bellows (or a fan for propane), an anvil and hammers, some tongs, some clamps or vices to hold the pieces you are working on, and last but not least some iron to work with. You will also need eye protection, a thick leather apron and gloves, and neighbours who don't mind the sound of you relentlessly pounding on metal.

Glass Blowing

Glass blowing is more than just a way of making homemade trinkets for your cousins bat mitzvah Bomboniere. (Bomboniere are those little gifts given by hosts on special occasions such as bat mitzvahs, weddings, baptisms, first communions or confirmations).

Glass blowing could be your passport to making some truly stunning artistic creations. Unique and colourful beads, bottles, bowls, glasses, goblets, light-shades, marbles, ornaments, paperweights, jewellery, vases and (for those who fancy a bit of hedonism) hookah pipes!

The equipment can be quite expensive, so if there is a studio near you I recommend you try it out before purchasing the necessary accoutrements. If you don't have access to a nearby studio and want to buy a basic kit to try it out you can start with a small torch, like a "Nortel Minor" which should cost less than $200. However, most experienced blowers recommend something with a wider flame, such as a "Major" or a "Red Max" (the wider the flame the greater the range of things you will be able to make), but either of these could set you back $400 or more. You will also need a supply of tank oxygen and propane along with the necessary regulators, and a good supply of glass tubes. You will also need eye protection and good ventilation at the very least. Glass blowing comes with a serious safety warning, molten glass is not something you want to be too casual with.

Lead Lighting

For those that like to see shards of coloured light dancing across their wall, but don't feel inclined to indulge in the necessary mind-altering substances to make it happen, lead lighting could be just the thing. Perfect for solemn religious buildings, period renovations and hippy hang outs, there is nothing sets off a room quite like bits of coloured glass stuck together with lead. Of course making your own is even better. You do not have to rely on one of the many lead light pattern books either. You can design something completely original and off the wall.

There are plenty of instructions and classes out there; you can even learn how to do it on YouTube. You will need some special equipment but nothing that is too expensive. Just some glass, a glasscutter and some lead. Once you get the hang of it, the only tricky part is deciding what patterns and colours to use.

Carpentry

Maybe you would like to be more like Jesus, or maybe you are just tired of all those chickens running around loose in the yard? You can kill those two birds with one stone by taking up carpentry and building yourself a chicken coop. From birdhouses to tables and benches, woodworking is an incredibly useful and rewarding skill to have; and if it turns out you are no good at it, remember that just like you Jesus was also a failed carpenter, so you're in mighty fine company!

Motor Mechanics

If you have no mechanical knowledge at all but still find that your car is far too reliable, maybe you could consider doing your own motor vehicle repairs. If you would like to be stranded by the roadside more often I highly recommend getting under the hood with a spanner and just randomly tinkering with things. If that seems like too much of an effort you could always sell your reliable car and buy that old rust bucket that you have always dreamed of. Sure, having an operational car may be practical but where's the fun in that?

Unlikely though it may seem, there are people who would actually like to improve the reliability of their cars. If this is you, you could always enrol yourself in a beginner's class in motor mechanics.

Restoration And Reinvention

You can restore and reinvent just about anything. Turn that dead car into a garden sculpture or a dog kennel! You can cut, hack, stencil, spray, sand, paint, glue and rivet any old junk into useful furniture, sculptural amazements or just plain curiosities. Re-purposing not only stretches the imagination, it makes old things new and exciting again.

Mosaics

Mosaic is one of the few art forms where you get to smash things and make things at the same time. With mosaics you can turn the remains of your last marital plate smashing festival into legitimate art supplies.

Typically made using pieces of broken tiles of various shapes, sizes and colours, mosaics can also be crafted using broken china, glass, coins, metal and plastics among other things. From the traditional Roman style

to the weird and wonderful works of Anton Gaudi, (the famous Artist and architect covered the streets of Barcelona in wild ceramic creations), mosaics are a true art form. It's well worth a visit to Barcelona if you need a little extra inspiration.

Gaudi Apartment Building In Barcelona

You can plan out your artwork or just go free form and see what comes out. You can make fantastical garden ornaments that will put your neighbour's gnomes to shame. You could even decorate the side of your house!

Hunters And Collectors

You can collect just about anything. The trick is to take it to the extreme. No matter what it is, if you take it totally over the top a news crew will want to film you and make a story out of it. A word of warning though, collecting can be obsessive so try not to pick something that will aggravate your neighbours or compromise your social cache too much. For example I would avoid collecting such things as dead cars, unspeakably druggy friends, medical waste, toenail clippings, old socks, used band-aids, unwashed underwear and household garbage. Such collections will not only turn you into a social liability but you will also become an environmental hazard. Conversely collecting things like old photographs, Barbie dolls, frog figurines, cookie jars, toy trains and movie posters will be viewed as a cute and curious hobby that may score you a slot in your local paper.

THE GREAT OUTDOORS

Tend Your Garden

In the immortal words of Voltaire, "tend your garden". Of course he was speaking figuratively, but it works just as well if you take it literally.

Gardening is incredibly grounding (yes, I know, very droll), and it really doesn't matter if you have a green thumb or not, everyone can grow something. If you are particularly inept when it comes to growing anything green, try planting a weed garden; they practically take care of themselves. You could even offer a lovely bouquet of weeds to your favourite neighbours to say a special thank you when their dog uses your front step as a toilet.

Seriously though, there is mounting research that suggests getting your hands into the dirt, and subsequently coming in contact with the soil bacteria Mycobacterium vaccae, can actually increase your serotonin levels. Serotonin not only strengthens the immune system, it is a noted happy chemical, and a natural anti-depressant, (whereas a lack of serotonin is one of the most noted causes of depression).

A lot of research has been emerging in recent years about how good dirt is for us, and how a dirt-deficiency in childhood could be contribute to conditions such as allergies, asthma and even some mental disorders. So next time you feel like getting down and dirty, don't hesitate. Get out there and get into it.

Grow Your Own Veggies

Fresh food is a total rip off in most supermarkets. First of all it's not usually that fresh, and it tends to be smothered in toxic pesticides. However if you like organic vegetables, saving money and grovelling in the dirt like a hippy, why not plant your own?

It takes less space and effort than you might think, and even if you don't have a yard you can still grow things in pots on a balcony. Here's an ingenious idea; some women in Africa suspended lengths of large PVC plumbers pipe on a rack. They closed off each end, cut holes in the top and drilled drainage holes in the bottom. They filled them with dirt and planted them out, and they were totally brilliant. They had a rack with about 7 of these pipes stacked up like a book shelf. They where growing all kinds of veggies and herbs, including lettuce, mint and strawberries.

Join A Community Garden

Maybe you fancy something a little more competitive (or social). What about a community garden? What better way to check out whether your squash is bigger than your neighbour's? Many municipalities have community gardens where locals can get an allotment, and if not you could always lobby your local authority to start one.

Community gardens are a stupendous option for anyone who has always wanted a garden but does not have the space. Many community gardens are full of avid swappers, which is just perfect for those who want a marrow and can give a spud. Whether it's swapping cuttings and seeds, chatting about manure (yes you can actually talk crap and have people really appreciate it), or sharing tips on pest control, there is so much to talk about in the garden. The fresh organic veggies are just a small part of being involved; it's the social aspect that is the real gift.

Go Wild With Topiary

For the uninitiated, topiary is the practice of clipping trees or shrubs into ornamental shapes. Contrary to what some people think topiary isn't just for formal gardens in manner houses. You can sculpt all kinds of amazing creatures out of common garden plants, (as was clearly demonstrated in the movie "Edward Scissor Hands"). Some people make such a theatrical feature of their garden that people come from miles around to see and photograph their creations. Whether you like a formal display, geometric shapes, Easter Island style totems, Dr. Seuss like trees or your own zoo full of topiary bears, elephants and giraffes, there is something for every taste. What's more, topiary is not expensive; all you need is a few hedging plants, a good set of pruning sheers and you are up and running. A few good shrubs could keep you going for years.

Bonsai Beauty

In the 6th century BC, Japanese students, dignitaries and Buddhist monks would bring back local ideas and practices from their visits to China. Thus the ancient Japanese art of Bonsai developed as an offshoot of the traditional Chinese practice of "penjing", (growing miniature trees in containers). Bonsai is a purely decorative form of cultivation, and its delicate beauty has been said to inspire quiet contemplation and wisdom among spiritual seekers.

Unlike outdoor trees, where the roots can spread out through the soil, the largest bonsai container is usually no bigger than a standard bucket. The largest bonsai will rarely exceed three feet tall, (with the vast majority being significantly smaller). Bonsai's are unquestionably high maintenance, and their successful cultivation can take some time to master. Many of its techniques, such as the selective removal of leaves, the wiring and clamping of branches, and detailed pruning and grafting are quite unique to the form. Working with bonsai's requires specialized tools, a reasonable knowledge of bonsai techniques, and good deal of patience. Regular watering, re-potting and fertilization are absolutely essential.

Cultivating bonsai's is the perfect hobby for anyone who loves plants, but hasn't got access to a garden. To start your own bonsai you will need an open flattish bowl with drainage and specimen of the plant you wish to work with. Many bonsai artists prefer to take a cutting from an old plant, as older plants tend to display a more aged aesthetic. Plants grown from seeds are rarely used.

Plant A Rose Garden

With their decorative and aromatic flowers roses are not just beautiful, they can make excellent burglar proofing when planted under your windows. After all, who in their right mind would brave a rose bush to try and pry open your window?

The successful cultivation of a rose garden takes planning and dedication. Whether you plant standard, long established varieties or try your hand at cross breeding and hybridisation there are a myriad of choices. There are even rose contests for the more competitively minded. And as an added bonus you will never be short of a cheap bouquet on Valentines day.

Learn How To Propagate Plants

Everyone knows that growing plants from seed can save a lot of cold hard cash, but it's not always easy. Yes, there are some seeds that you can just throw on the ground and they will grow like crazy. Unfortunately most of them are weeds; but there are some flowers, such as nasturtiums, alysums and gypsophila for example, that are almost impossible to fail with. That said, if your gardening prowess is so challenged that your plants literally die on the way to the car the moment you step outside the nursery, you might want to try gardening with plants that don't cost you anything.

Growing plants from cuttings and rhizomes is often much easier than trying to raise seedlings, and it is a great way to start up a garden with no financial outlay at all. Many plants, such as succulents, pelargoniums, geraniums, agapanthus and chrysanthemums (just to name a few) are so easy to grow from cuttings that your success is practically guaranteed. Some succulents are so simple to propagate that if you brush past them and snap a bit off, (and don't pick it up), you will have a new plant in a couple of weeks!

If you see a plant you particularly like in someone's garden why not knock on their door and ask for a cutting. It's a great way to meet other garden oriented people in your neighbourhood. Gardeners tend to be very generous with each other when it comes to swapping cuttings and rhizomes (root divisions), so you could not only end up with a blooming garden but a whole lot of new friends to boot! YouTube is full of easy to follow tutorials on how to strike cuttings, and I gaurantee you, it's easier than you think.

Raise Some Chickens

While you might not win the love of your neighbours with a cow or sheep in your garden, you might be able to keep some chickens. Not only will you enjoy fresh wholesome, cruelty free eggs, but your dogs will just love chasing them around the yard. There are a lot of varieties of chickens to choose from, and they all have different temperaments and abilities; however some of them can be quite homely.

If you are rather shallow or overly image conscious I recommend you ignore the clever ones with good personalities and stick to the air-headed, good-looking chicks. A few drop dead gorgeous "trophy" chickens in your coop will do wonders for your standing at the local agricultural show. While I definitely don't condone such behaviour, if you prefer your chicks "really hot" you could make like Henry the 8th and chop off their heads and cook them. (Although in fairness, I don't think he cooked any of his decapitates).

Whether you want them for dinner or for their eggs, or just for their company chickens are a wonderful addition to any home.

Pack A Picnic

If you are on budget but still want million dollar views with your lunch, there is no better way than packing a picnic lunch. You can picnic just about anywhere. Whether you choose to chow down in a manicured park, at the zoo, on the beach, by the riverbank, on the lakeside, by a waterfall or in the city square, picnicking has some big advantages over your local restaurant. For a start, there is no chance there won't be something you like on the menu. You can begin eating whenever you like, as you don't have to wait for the chef to deal with the thirty people that just walked in ahead of you. You don't have to worry about the loud bore at the next table, or withering eye-rolls of arroagant waiters; and you don't have to put up with the selection of Casiotone polkas blasting out from their speakers.

Hobby Farming

If you love the idea of casually working the land and you are not looking to reap vast financial rewards hobby farming could be the perfect solution. Even if you are not keen on selling up and moving to the country, you may still be able to grow some veggies, keep some poultry, rabbits, or even a bee hive if your local authority will permit it. According to Wikipedia, you only need an acre of land to support a couple of milking goats or some pigs. Even if you just love the rural lifestyle but don't want to do much work at all hobby farming, (or homesteading as it is sometimes called), can provide for you. There are plenty of crops, like olives, that require very little in the way of ongoing maintenance; so you can just sit back and let nature do the work.

Go Camping, Or Glamping!

Camping is a great way to commune with nature and it can be done at any level. Whether you go wild with a pop up tent and a backpack, or prefer a few more of the rudimentary creature comforts, like beds, cookers and solar powered TV's, camping can accommodate. Why not try the new craze in camping that is taking the world by storm? Glamping, (or "glamorous camping") is a luxury high-end experience especially designed for those that want the escapism, recreation and adventure of camping along with the style and comfort of a five star hotel.

If camping has never really been your thing, but you like the idea of living like a wealthy Bedouin for a few days, glampling might be for you? In some cities they even have rooftop glamping, where you can gaze at the stars while sleeping in a luxury open tent on the top of your local skyscraper.

Although we are only now rediscovering its joys, glamping is not a new concept. There are many noted historical examples. In the sixteenth century, the Duke of Atholl prepared an extreme glamping experience in the Scottish Highlands for King James V's visit. He raised a veritable village of lavish tents and stuffed them with all the luxuries one would expect to find in a royal palace. The Ottomans where also noted glampers. They used to have dedicated teams of artisans travel with their armies just to look after the opulent tents of the imperial generals.

SOCIAL

Pubs And Clubs

While some pubs and bars are clearly depressing pits full of sticky carpet and slot machines, others play host to social groups that regularly meet to eat drink and be merry. There are bars with loyal locals that are a bit like a club, and there are countless actual clubs that have their meetings in local pubs. There are clubs for just about everything imaginable, from chess to cross-dressing. Whatever your proclivity there will be a pub or club out there brimming with like-minded folk that can help you bring your social needs and interests together.

If, for some strange reason, there isn't the club you are looking for in your local area, it is very easy to start one these days. The website "www.meetup. com" operates across the world, with "meetups" for everything from cycling, eating, photography, film buffs, fancy dress, dancing, camping, Kung-Fu, opera, quite literally anything! You can find clubs close to your area, or start a club by signing up and posting a notice. So simple!

Become A Quiz Whiz

What better place to show off that vast accumulation of knowledge than at the local pub quiz? The pub quiz is a long-standing institution, and the perfect environment for smart arses and knows-it-alls. There are not too many places that you can show off how clever you are, eat pub food, and get hammered while you are about it. What could be better?

Chess Clubs

Chess is a wonderful game for those who prefer their warfare cerebral and bloodless rather than violent and visceral, and if you do it in the park you can get your vitamin D hit while you are at it. Chess players tend to be a very earnest and serious lot. Some players are so uptight about winning that they take a small eternity to make a move and get quite sullen and sulky if they lose.

If you are into looking overly intelligent, brooding chin scratching gestures, and generally psyching out your opponents a chess club could be perfect for you. However if you feel like a mindless belly laugh, then maybe not.

Start A Slow Cooking Club

Slow cooking is where it's at these days. Many people are starting their own cooking circles, where once a week a group of people get together to cook something adventurous. Each member of the circle is tasked with bringing certain ingredients and making one part of the meal. While cooking there is much chat and social time, with a large slice of the conversation dedicated to unusual recipes, or what fruits or vegetables should be included in next week's offering. The whole process may take several hours, several bottles of vino, and several hungry mouths to complete.

Vintage Car Clubs

Vintage car enthusiasts are totally nuts when it comes to their cars. Very few parents love their children as much as a car buff will love his mint condition pink and white 1952 Chevy convertible with the tail fins. Car people will abandon all sense of fiscal restraint when it comes to the loving care and maintenance of their prized ride. The level of auto obsession, not to mention spit and polish that goes into getting a vintage car ready for a rally day is simply staggering. If you want to get your partner out of the house and into the garage this is definitely an activity to encourage.

Motorcycle Clubs

Motorcycle clubs come in all shapes and sizes. They are not all the hairy, unwashed outlaws of popular mythology; some are rich and ultra clean. Many Harley riders spend hours polishing their bikes, their leathers, and of course their helmets!

There are clubs out there that are specially for those that no longer have the kids at home, like the Ulysses Club (Australia) a social club for riders over 40, whose membership is dedicated to "growing old disgracefully", or the more family friendly Older Bikers Riding Club that have branches right across the USA.

Then there are your more up market clubs. My husband actually belongs to two clubs; the Ducati club, (a bigger bunch of "mature" successful business people I have yet to meet), and a smaller local club that organises charity events for the local children's hospital.

Film Clubs

If you are a genre nut, or love films of a particular era you could either join or start your own film club. In this day and age, where most people's televisions are bigger than their childhood home, it's not hard to find a venue with a big enough screen to accommodate your weekly offerings. If you want to spread it out beyond your own circle of friends you could always post a notice on local blogs or www.meetup.com and bring a few new bodies into your club; and if you all drink like fish you could probably get the local pub to host it for free!

Join The Medievalists

So lords and ladies, if jousting, lutes, pointy hats and codpieces are your thing the Society for Creative Anachronisms is definitely for you.

If you just love heraldry, chivalry, archery, fancy dress, gnawing meat off the bone, singing madrigals and camping in boggy fields with other medievalists, the SCA has got you covered. These people are FUN, and totally wacky!

Book Clubs

In my limited experience book clubs are excellent places for intellectuals and quasi intellectuals to eat cake and bitch about their partners. With a book club not only are you spared the trauma of deciding which book to read, you can trust the others in the group to reliably tell you what you should to think of the book once you have read it. This can take a lot of pressure off, as you no longer need to form your own opinion. When someone asks what you thought of the book, you can simply parrot the group's assessment. If you do happen to have an opinion that differs from the group it is better to keep it to yourself. Book clubs are a veritable hotbed of "groupthink" and any deviation from the standard line is usually seriously frowned upon.

What's Your Game?

Games are totally underrated! You can learn an extraordinary amount playing games, and I'm not just talking about honing your game skills; it's the social, interactive aspects that are totally fascinating. Through games we learn how to be humble in victory and gracious in defeat. We are all told from the time we were old enough to listen, *"it's not whether you win or lose, it's how you play the game"*.

Of course everyone knows winning is the whole point, and that oft repeated platitude is merely there to provide some kind of balm for the losers. But even so, the fear of suffering a humiliating defeat is simply not strong enough to stem our pursuit of irrelevant victories. Whether we admit it or not we all love to play games and we all love to win; even if that means taking our turn as total losers from time to time.

Card Games

Fortunes and friendships have been made and lost over a game of cards. From the meditative isolation of solitaire to the simmering undertones of an intimate bridge party, our card-playing obsession has endured

throughout the centuries. From strip poker to black jack, cards have been used as a prelude to romance, a means to fleece the unwary and a simple way to pass the time.

These days there is so much more on offer than just the poker, black jack, bridge, euchre, rummy or cribbage found in "Hoyle's" book of games. There are many new card games available, and some of them are even quite risqué. Take "f**ktionary" for example. (Yes, it's a real thing). In f**ktionary, players compete to come up with the lewdest answer they can to game questions. Along a similar, but slightly more challenging lines is "Mobscenity". In which you select two "word" cards, and combine those words into one phrase, and then obscenely define what that phrase might mean.

There are, of course, modern card games that are still rather quirky but not quite so vulgar, such as "Guillotine". Set in the French revolution, you play rival guillotine operators and compete for the most valuable heads. Or "Gloom" where the goal is to make your character suffer as much as possible before they die.

Other best selling card games include "Cards against humanity", "Exploding Kittens", "Uno", "Joking Hazard" and my perennial favourite "Munchkin". Munchkin is a strategy card game that has kept my husband and his friends out of my hair for hours at a stretch. Munchkin is so loved and successful by those that play that is now has something like 6,000 expansion packs available. If you're looking for something more intricate and involved than a quick, easy game, Munchkin is the one for you. But be careful though, once you get into it you could become addicted.

Traditional Games

While no one really wants to spend hours doing a Jackson Pollack jigsaw, there are plenty of traditional games that have remained staggeringly popular throughout the ages. Chess, Backgammon, Mah Jong, Chinese Checkers, Drafts, Dominoes, Battle Ships, Hangman, Chess, Yatzee, Jacks, Snakes and Ladders, Ludo and Lego, just to name a few.

Board Games

Unlike computer games board games give you the opportunity to really use your game face. You can psyche out your opponents with your laser like death stare, or try lulling them into a false sense of security with a slightly befuddled look. Board games are like hand to hand combat for the non-combatant.

Some board games are clearly better than others. Mastermind, Dungeons and Dragons, Risk, Cluedo, Pictionary, Trivial Pursuit, Jenga, Connect four, Sorry, Go, Scattergories, Othello, Mousetrap, Kerplunk, Boggle, Twister, Operation, Hungry hippo and Scrabble, are all amazingly great!

Monopoly on the other hand has always been a bit of a worry. My entire childhood memory of Monopoly was that it generally began well, but pretty soon descended into one player exhibiting all the voracious greed of a Russian oligarch. Everyone else would become increasingly despondent, until finally someone petulantly tossed their piece across the room and declared they weren't playing anymore. (Not really my idea of fun).

Dance The Night Away

Tango anyone? Did you know that in Buenos Aires you can see 70 year-olds tangoing in the street at two in the morning? From the spiced up Latin rhythms of the cha cha, to the refined formality of a waltz dancing is

a great way to get yourself into the arms of a stranger (or your partner if you prefer).

Whether you love a sizzling samba, a jumping jive, a punk pogo or a mindless macarena, there is a dance for practically every taste and musical preference, Hit the mosh pit, form a tap dancing troop, or go strictly ballroom. If you are feeling particularly sexy and adventurous you could even try the waist-trimming roll of a belly dance class to get you moving. Even if you can't dance you can still hit the floor; just make up your own moves. Who knows, you might even enjoy hurling yourself about with a random flailing of limbs. Whichever way you do it, dancing is a great way to get fit and have fun; and if you really are truly awful at it just think of the joyous laughter your moves can give to others. So why not get off the couch and get your endorphins pumping? What could be more social than dancing?

GOING SOLO

Solo Games

Rubik's Cubes, Crosswords, Sudoku, Solitaire, Free-cell, Word Finder puzzles and Totem Tennis are all great ways to fill in a few odd minuets, or

even sharpen up your grey matter when travelling solo. My favourite game for exercising the mind when I am on my own is "Boggle". Boggle is not strictly speaking a solo game, but I like to challenge myself. It is played by shaking a covered tray of 16 cubic dice, each with a different letter printed on each of its sides. The dice fall into a tray where only the top letter of each cube is visible. You have three-minutes in which to search for words that can be constructed from the letters of sequentially adjacent cubes, ("adjacent" cubes are those horizontally, vertically, and diagonally neighbouring). Of course, being a word person I love Boggle almost as much as Scrabble!

Computer Games

Computer games can be as simple as solitaire, or they can be highly complex virtual worlds in which you can interact with millions of other players in real time, all from the privacy of your own room. Whether you are playing a game for one, challenging a computer generated opponent or entering a virtual world, like 'World of Warcraft' to 'Second Life' millions of people log on every day to play their favourite games. Beware though, it can be highly addictive!

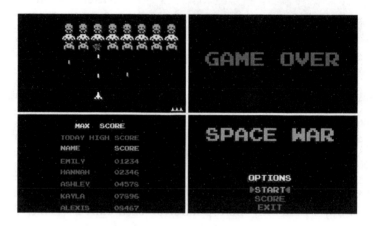

Build A Model Railway

If you ever wanted to play God by creating your own personal world, then building a model railway could be just the thing. It's the ultimate megalomanica's playground! You can design and entrie intricate world,

complete with trees, grass, people, animals, shops, cars, stations, bridges, tracks and trains; and you are its undisputed overlord. The people go wherever you say they go. The trains run whenever tyou say they run. If anything displeases you, you can simply make like Gmoez Adams and blow it up!

MUSICAL

Not only is music is one of the most enjoyable aspects of life, there is mounting evidence that playing music helps to keep the mind sharp. Most sensory inputs only activate one localized area in the brain, but music sparks neural activity all over the place, simultaneously firing up the areas of the brain that process sound, memory, attention, language, sight, touch and more. Music brings these separate centres together in a way few other experiences can.

Learn A Musical Instrument

For those who would like to try their hand at playing an instrument you will be pleased to know it is not as difficult as you might think. You can go the self-taught route, take some lessons, or even sign up for an online course. The wonderful thing about playing a musical instrument is that it makes you feel totally euphoric; and once you have your instrument it costs you absolutely nothing. These days, with advanced robotic manufacturing, you can find a wide variety of cheap, quality instruments, either on EBay or on the High St. There has never been a better time to get yourself that musical instrument you have always dreamed of.

If you love music you can quite literally play for several hours every day. Not only does playing music provide countless hours of totally absorbing activity, it boosts your levels of dopamine, (a chemical that regulates the pleasure and rewards centres within the brain). It's a far better high than throwing back a few beers.

Oh, and as an added bonus a lot of musical instruments give you a fair workout into the bargain; and not just the drums, playing guitar or piano can burn a lot of calories too.

Sing A Song

Whether you want to join a band, a choir, or go chanting in a Hindu temple, singing is an incredible feel good experience, and it's amazingly good for your health too. It will keep your endorphins pumping while keeping your lungs fit and active. Even if you are not up for singing in a public you can still have an amazingly good time warbling in the shower.

If you fancy your self as a bit of a crooner you could download some karaoke midi files and invite your friends over for a sing along. You can find a midi file for practically any song you can think of somewhere on the net, so you should have no trouble finding your favourites. Most times you can find the lyrics on Google as well.

"http://www.midaoke.com/" has an enormous catalogue of songs for free.

A midi file is a backing track that will usually play back on your computer. Although you may need to Google and download a midi file player.

However, if you need a bit more confidence to get you out of your shell you might consider taking a lesson or two. Whether you want to sing opera, heavy metal or yodelling you way through the day, there is no need to keep that voice hidden in the bathroom. You can either find a teacher, (although lessons can stretch the budget), or sign up for an online course, where one payment buys you a course of lessons for life.

I recommend you check out the Singing Zone:

"https://www.thesingingzone.com/sing-with-freedom" (I don't have any association with this vendor, and get no kick back from sales).

Alternately, if you have a sense of humour about it, you could always turn your self into a comedic parody of a singer. That way you can have a successful singing career, (even if you are way over 40), and you don't have to be any good at all. Just Google up "Wing singer", or "Margarita Pracatan" and check these ladies out. If they can do it, so can you! (Seriously, check them out; they are jaw dropping!)

Join A Choir

Choirs are a wonderfully social option, and a great way to ease into the sing of things; after all there is safety in numbers. If you like the gospel gowns and love listening to everyone else singing around you, but are worried that people might start writhing in pain as soon as you open your mouth, you could always do what my mother does and just mouth the words. It's not really cheating if you are having fun.

Open Mic Nights

Music is highly social. Even if you are not ready to join a band there is usually an open mic night or a jam session or two in every town. And even if you don't feel up to getting up on stage yourself it's an excellent place to get involved with the local scene and meet people that you can maybe jam with at home.

Write A Song

I love song writing. I have been doing it since I was about 8 years old and have written hundreds of songs over my lifetime. I even taught a class in it once. You don't need to be proficient at playing an instrument; in fact you really don't need to know anything much about music at all. You don't even need three chords, as there are plenty of fabulous two chord songs about!

The main thing with song writing is to let it flow. It's about getting the lyrics together in a way that matches the tone and tempo of the music. There are many software programs – like the Real Book app, Band in a Box, or Garage Band- that can take care of the music side for you, leaving you free to pen anything from a love song to punk anthem.

It really is dead easy. Just bang together a quick computer backing track, or make a slight adjustment to the chords of a song you like and you are free to warble and express your self until something good falls out.

I recommend trying to write the WORST song you possibly can to get you started. It's a great fun exercise, and you can compare your best worst efforts with a friend.

Once you have done something truly awful and shared it over a laugh, you are then free to express yourself without inhibition; letting those 95 truly rancid ideas flow through to get to the 5 good ones! As soon as you are comfortable with the idea that not every word you write has to be brilliant, you can have an absolute ball with song writing. If you let 100 ideas flow out, chances are at least one or two of them will be good. Like this, line after line, build up your words and melody until voilà! A song!

Once you have a few songs written you could book a studio and record them, or just lay them down on your computer. You could even upload them to iTunes for sale, or convert one into your ring tone.

If you like a touch of evil fun, you could proudly present a copy of your most putrid songs to your kids for Christmas. Tell them how proud of it you are, and earnestly ask them if they like it? For the record, this is exactly the sort of thing my husband does to me on a regular basis, (and for some unfathomable reason I always fall for it). Anyway, as long as you don't leave them squirming too long, it's good for a laugh!

LITERARY

Dive Into Literature

The pen is mightier than the sword. Which is rather convenient when you take into account the high price and relative inaccessibility of swords; and the fact that you can buy a pen at the local shop for under a dollar.

Of course, these days writing with a keyboard is considerably quicker and easier. But no matter what means you use to get your words out, you can weave together whole worlds from pure imagination. Your words can be challenging, inspiring, confronting, or whimsical, anything really. Whether it's the story of Fred the flying amoeba or your personal political manifesto, there is no reason to keep your thoughts hidden from the page indefinitely. Get writing!

Write A Novel Or A Screen Play

Statistically speaking 100% of people have a great idea for a novel or screenplay. (If you don't believe me take a straw poll at the next party you attend). This means that simply by virtue of being human you must have at least one story you are burning to tell. Why not take the opportunity to get yours out onto the page? You don't have to produce a word-perfect first draft. You simply have to let the ideas flow. The spit and polish can come later, when you get into editing. There are some wonderful books to help you learn how to construct a story and get you started. I recommend Joseph Campbell's "The Hero's Journey" or Robert McKee's "Story".

Write A Short Story

If you are too lazy or just too impatient to write a whole novel why not go for the speedy alternative and pen a short story. Did you know that the master of creepy and weird, Edgar Allen Poe mostly wrote short stories? In fact he only ever wrote one novel. But seriously, short stories are a wonderfully liberating form. You can explore the intricate nuances of a single idea in one succinct piece, or put together a collection to explore a theme from several different angles.

Start A Blog Or A Vlog

Blogging is a fantastic way to have to your say. Doesn't matter what the topic, if you blog it, someone will read it! A blog is an online journal/publication that is usually (but not always) dedicated to a particular topic. There are many websites that will host your blog for FREE. One of the best and most popular is Wordpress. There are lots of online tutorials on Youtube so if you are not sure how to do it just Google up the information you need. Just visit "www.wordpress.com" and sign up for a free account

If you are craving more fame, and would like to turn yourself into a celebrity cult figure you could go wild on your very own video blog (called a "vlog"). The idea is the same as a blog but instead of writing you talk into a video or camera and upload it to Youtube. People love wild and weird Vlogs. You can go so much further than with just the written word, you can wear strange outfits, build yourself a set and let your personality shine through in the most direct way possible.

Send Letters To The Editor

If you have plenty of opinions to share around this is a really fun activity. You can take issue with a particular columnist, (some of them make it so easy), or you can just criticize and condemn with utter impunity.

If you find your letters are not making it into the mainstream papers as often as you would like, you could always try your hand at blog comments. Comments are a great medium for passionately opinionated people who don't feel up to writing and maintaining their own blogs; they are also a fabulous outlet for habitual trolls.

Write Your Biography

Turn all those priceless anecdotes your family no longer want to hear into literary gold. If you are living a fascinating life why not share the unique intricacies of your personal story with the world? If you don't want to take the time off from your adventures you could always dictate it and have it transcribed, or you could even hire a ghost-writer. Upwork is full of them. www.upwork.com

Get Down With A Poetry Slam

From the Shakespearean highbrow of "Shall I compare thee to a summer day?",to the immortal bathroom classic "Here I sit broken hearted...." Poetry is everywhere.

From the humble limerick to a wistful haiku, from gangster rap to a lover's sonnet there are so many forms and meters to poetry. You could write just about anything and declare it poetry; there simply are no rules. (Well, except for the forms that have rules that is, which of course is most forms, but you don't have to obey them!)

When I was a teenager I joined a colourful band of "street poets", aged 14-80. We used to print out our poetry and hand it out for free to passers by on the street. We handed out hundreds of poems everyday and it never failed to raise a smile.

Of course, there is no law that says you have to hand out the fruits of your literary labour for free. I once purchased a spontaneously written poem from a guy with an old typewriter who was "poetry busking" on Fisherman's Wharf (in San Francisco). My immediate thought was that every city and town NEEDS someone doing this. Maybe that someone could be you?

Read Through Your Bookshelf

Everyone has that list of books they always wanted to read but never had the time. Well, now you do! Why not take some time to relax and work your way through that library that has been gathering dust on the bookcase.

Join The Local Library

This is kind of a no brainer. Libraries will lend you books to read for free, which is amazing. There is no excuse for not joining and making use of the incredible resource. Even if you're not that into books, many libraries have all the latest magazines on racks so you can read them for free. They also tend to have some of the best notice boards around. Anything going on in the neighbourhood, from free concerts to free medical screenings will usually find it's way onto the library notice board.

EDUCATIONAL

Give Yourself A First, Second Or Third Degree

OK, your friends may think you are already a bit of a know-it-all, but why not add some letters to your title. BA, MBA, MA, Phd? It's all good stuff at a dinner party! If you enrol yourself in an undergrad class you may even get to hang out with some lovely folk who are still young enough to know everything. Lucky you!

It doesn't have to be seriously expensive Ivy League study either. There are plenty of online universities, scholarships and community colleges out there offering affordable or even free studies. In fact Germany just made its University tuition free for everyone, no matter what country you come from.

Also many colleges and universities now offer courses on line. Why not check out "Stanford Online" (online.stanford.edu/), or EdX (https://www.edx.org/) which provides information and links to some of the best free university courses from places like MIT, Berkeley UC, Caltech, Dartmouth, Princeton, Cornell, Boston University, Imperial College London, Australian National University, The University of Tokyo plus a whole lot more.   Many of them even offer free courses. For example it's well worth checking out what is available from the Harvard open learning initiative, (www.extension.harvard.edu/open-learning-initiative).

Self Educate

Many of the smartest and most successful people in the world didn't finish high school. Which really isn't all that surprising, as formal education is not always a great option for a curious mind. If you are an unconventional thinker, have interests that lie outside the mainstream, or simply can't afford formal study, you can always do it yourself.

Maybe you are curious as to how the assassination of one Arch Duke led to the deaths of over 37 million people? Perhaps you have wondered what Einstein was talking about when he coined the term "Spooky action at a distance"? Maybe you feel a pressing need to brush up on your knowledge of the mating habits of the sea cucumber? Even for those who don't have the Internet at home, there are still public libraries, and many of them have computers and free Internet access, so you can quench that nagging thirst for knowledge.

Join A Debating Club

Not only is debating great for anyone who loves a good argument, it is seriously educational. When you are given a position to argue you will need to do significant research to mount a compelling case. But it's not just your research that can teach you a thing or two, you get to hear all the information and interpretations brought to subject by the other debaters. It's is a great way to stretch your thinking out beyond your own assumed positions and opinions.

Sit In On A Free Lecture

Many universities and colleges have a regular program of free public lectures. They usually try to present on a wide range of topics, so you shouldn't find it too hard to find one that appeals. Just recently my husband and I attended a fascinating series of six lectures on astrophysics. They even provided tea and biscuits (cookies???). We learned some interesting dinner party facts and got to meet some interesting people during the break. Check out the tertiary institutions in your area, I am sure they will have something on offer that is too good to miss.

Know Nothing And Do It Anyway

AKA the school of fake it till you make it. Just do it. What ever it is have a go, you will very soon learn what works and what doesn't. Often those that forego any knowledge or formal training will come up with new techniques and innovative ways to do things that they never would have thought of if they had been trained. Abandoning accepted protocol is so much fun. Why not throw away the recipe and just guess, why not colour outside the lines? Admittedly the results may be a disaster but equally you might find yourself becoming the originator of a new form. Nothing ever got invented by following the pattern.

Get on line and check out "the bush mechanics", a group of inspired folk from the Australian outback who live in such a remote location that they have learnt how to use things like tree branches to fix the broken axle in their car.

POLITICAL

There is nothing quite like the cut and thrust of a good debate. Whether it's hurling insults across the chamber, or banging fists at the dinner table, politics is a passionate pursuit. If you want to tax the billionaires, champion the middle class, kick the poor or save the planet then politics is definitely for you.

Join A Political Party

If you genuinely want to do more to further your own ideals, how about joining a political party? Don't be fooled by the term "party". I can assure there is nothing light or frivolous about these parties. Yes, it's true their primary obsession may be handing out leaflets, but they are also pretty good for sharpening up the old Machiavellian manoeuvres.

Why not start your own party? A political party is a fabulous choice for anyone who loves power, intrigue and indulging themselves in incessant arguments.

Go Green!

If you just love being self-righteous, shaming your friends, or calling out total strangers on their wasteful and selfish ways, then going green is going to be heaps of fun for you.

Not only will going green save you money, help reduce pollution and preserve the living environment, you will get to glare scornfully at those ignorant folk who failed to bring their own bags to the supermarket. You can even switch other people's lights off in the middle of the day and give them earnest sermons about how wasteful they are. The best part is that you will be right, and they will know it.

Whether it's chaining yourself to a tree, lobbying to save the whale or choosing to ride your bicycle instead of taking the car, going green gives you heaps of opportunity for activism. From petitioning food giants to reduce their packaging to getting big gas to stop fracking, there is literally a whole world of opportunity for the modern greenie.

Lobby For Your Cause

Does the idea of making a difference in the world appeal to you? Maybe you think that the world has far too many of those pesky wind farms and you want to do something about it. Maybe you want to stop those poor coal miners becoming endangered? Well why not start a lobby group to advocate for them?

There are so many great causes to choose from. Lowering taxes for billionaires and multinational corporations, (although to be fair they have well established gaggle of lobbyists already working on their cause); striking Darwin's theory of evolution from the high school curriculum; you can lobby for practically anything,

Lobbyists have helped to change many laws all over the country. You don't need to have any special skills, knowledge or intelligence to lobby, but you do need to be passionate about your cause. What's more, when you surround yourself with other lobbyists who share the exact same ideas and opinions as you, you can avoid ever being challenged on your beliefs. Happy days!

VOYEURISTIC

I Like To Watch

Watching, viewing, looking, leering, peering, peeking, gawking, gazing, glimpsing, glancing, staring, perving or just keeping an eye on things. The pleasures of the human eye are immeasurable. Whether one is staring into a flickering fire, cheering on the game, sauntering through the Guggenheim, taking in a show or trolling the Internet for questionable content, simply watching things is one of our greatest human joys.

Go Train Spotting

Train spotting is bags of fun for obsessives. Spotters spend countless hours trying to land an eyeball on all kinds of different types of rolling stock. It is not uncommon for train spotters to form small prides and exchange notes on their spots, and where and when they saw them.

Many spotters like to photograph the carriage and serial numbers or record them in log books. Unfortunately, due to the fact that every second person is planning to blow up some public utility or the other these days, photographing trains has become somewhat frowned on, (and doubly so

if you happen to be wearing a burqa at the time); but you shouldn't let the spectre of being indefinitely detained as a terrorist suspect deter you. Train spotting really is fabulous. If you would like a lower risk alternative, try visiting a train museum. You can spot all kinds of old world rolling stock without fear of becoming a terror suspect.

Enjoy A Spot Of Bird Watching

Bird watching first appeared as a gentleman's pastime in Victorian times, where observing birds for purely aesthetic reasons was considered a luxury of the well fed. Everyone else viewed them as a potential meal.

Bird watching is an excellent pastime for those with voyeuristic tendencies, as you can quite legitimately get about with binoculars slung around you neck without raising any suspicions. Thankfully not all bird watchers have a proclivity for taxidermy, which is the somewhat gruesome habit of stuffing and mounting dead animals.

Become A Star Gazer

If you love telescopes, observatories and cloudless desert nights, stargazing could be for you. Maybe you're worried that you might be a bit narcissistic and self- important? Well nothing can make you feel quite as insignificant as the sheer vastness of the cosmos. But apart from its obviously humbling aspects, astronomy is also a great hobby for vampires, (or anyone else that finds they are unable to face the daylight hours).

However, if you would rather inflate, rather than deflate your ego, astronomy can help with that too! How about having a star named after you? (Or your significant other). Admittedly paying to have this done is largely a scam by unscrupulous Internet entrepreneurs, but you don't have to line their pockets. You can just pick a star, make up a name, print up a certificate and hang it on your wall, (or tie it up with a pretty ribbon and give it to your partner).

Check Out Museums And Galleries

Museums and galleries are well worth travelling for. You should see the works of Van Gough, Leonardo DaVinci and the fossilized remains of a trilobite at least once in your life. It is simply staggering what they have in museums, it's like walking into another world. Mini snuff boxes from the court of Queen Elizabeth the first, the Apollo moon capsule, the Elgin Marbles, Rodin's Thinker, three thousand year old Greek pottery, the Ishtar gates, really silly animatronic dinosaurs; all of these things I have seen in museums.

A tree made of guns, a Gaultier bustier, the terracotta army, Jackson Pollack's Blue poles, Andy Warhol soup cans, and some esoteric installation piece by Claudia Luenig (my incredible artist friend from Vienna), all of this has been served up to my eyeballs in Galleries. Mind boggling ideas, staggering inspirations, incredible artistic skill, it's all out there on show in your local gallery.

Do The Zoo

While I love looking at the lions, seeing the seals, gazing at gazelles, taking in the tigers and meandering past the meerkats, going to the zoo is always a tainted pleasure for me. Fortunately many modern zoos have gone to great pains to make wonderful enclosures and naturalistic environments for the animals, but it is tragic that animals that should be free are locked in cages.

The sad truth is that we have made a bit of a mess of things and many of these animals now need our help to survive. As we've messed up their world I think the least we can do is lend our support to their survival; and

one of the best ways we can do this is to visit our local zoos. The ticket price will help fund efforts to stave off extinction and disease, so it's well worth it. There is a great deal to be learned from our animal friends, and what better way to learn it than to pay them a visit?

Take In A Show, Or Two!

From top end productions to local theatre groups, arts festivals and street performers, most cities and towns have a wealth of entertainment on offer. Sure you can lash out on a Broadway show, but that's far from all that's out there. Try exploring the off-beat world of fringe theatre and off Broadway style selections in your local area.

Whether it's a burlesque cabaret, a stand up comedy night, a theatre sports round or an amateur Tennessee Williams play, live shows are exciting. If you want to make sure that you don't miss out, why not sign up for an entertainment company's mailing list, so they can let you know when something fun is on. www.citysearch.com usually has local listings for all kinds of things.

Film Festivals

If you love long agonizing films about awful people, films that don't have any discernible plot line, or even films that you just don't understand, then your local film festival might be just the thing.
I know it is difficult to find these types of films at the local cinema, but don't worry film festivals are full of them! While there are some festivals that specialize in specifically

"entertaining" genres, (like comedy or science fiction), the vast majority are totally dedicated to wrist-slashingly turgid dramas that are almost too painful to watch. Festival films have even been known to induce audience members to spontaneously suicide, so this is no place to go if you are emotionally fragile.

But seriously while about 80-90% of festival films may be a tad on the torturous side, it's the 10-20%, those gems that you won't see anywhere else that make it well worth taking a punt on the price of ticket. There is also that special sense of community you feel when you sit in the dark with other people totally absorbed in a story. It's like being gathered around an ancient camp fire staring into the flickering light while someone weaves a magical tale.

Enjoy Some Live Music

Live music is not all big concerts or sweaty teens in mosh pits. From head banging death metal to a discerning classical ear, there is something for everyone. Whether you choose to take in some west coast rock, funk, soul, jazz, blues or folk there are plenty of venues that cater for people of all shapes, sizes and ages. Check out the venues in your local area or head off to a concert in the big city. Whatever your thing is, I can assure you it is out there just waiting to hit your ears.

PERFORMING

Show Me

Performing artists have been pushing the boundaries of human understanding throughout recorded history. Whether you resonate with the tragic humanity of Shakespeare and Chekov, the startling visuals of Cirque d' solei, or the pulsing lights and wild beats of your local DJ, there are so many things out there to see and hear. Participating in a live show can open up your mind to new possibilities. It can smash your fears and change the way you see, hear and process information. Once you lose your fear, you will find every live performance you experience has the capacity to alter your perceptions; both of yourself and the world around you. Getting involved in the performing arts is one of the best ways to stretch the bounds of your imagination.

Lights, Camera, Action

Your relationship with film doesn't have to be limited to just being a consumer. If you have a megaphone, a riding crop, a director's chair, a video camera or a smart phone, then you are well on the way to becoming a film-maker. You won't even need actors if you have a cat, (although just like a temperamental actor your cat will probably refuse to take direction, demand better food and agitate for a bigger trailer).

Si Fi, horror, romance, comedy, a heart warming family birthday? Whatever the genre you can have a go. Write a script. Turn your spare room, the local park, or the local pub into your movie set. Ask around, I am sure you will find no shortage of amateur actors who would love to star in your film. Maybe documentary or cinema veritie is your thing? In which case just grab your camera, go people watching and film life as it happens.

Most computers come with some form of free movie editing software such as i-movie, and if not there is plenty of free movie editing software that can be downloaded from the Internet. There's plenty of royalty free music you can use in programs like Garage Band, so you can get a cool soundtrack going without worrying about whether you just became a pirate.

There are so many ways to get your videos and films seen. Not only are there regular short film nights in most cities and large towns, there are hundreds of short film festivals throughout the world that you can enter your film into.

Move Over Ted Turner

If you decide to create your own films or videos, what better way to share them with the world than putting them up online? Why not start your own YouTube channel? (In case there is anyone out there who doesn't know this already, YouTube is a video-sharing site where people from all over the world post their own video and films for people to see). It is very easy to make your own YouTube channel and it costs you nothing. You could even make your own television-style talk show, news and op-ed show or even a craft, hobby or cooking show.

Once you have established your channel you can ask well-known locals or semi-famous people to guest on your show. You never know, your channel might become a huge hit around the world! You tube now has paid advertising so if you make a popular show you could also end up supplementing your income.

Make Some Magic

Magicians have been delighting audiences for centuries. Of course, these days they are mostly found at kid's birthday parties, but that is no reason not to learn a few tricks. If you get your performance skills up you could even put on the odd show. Admittedly, a lot of magic tricks require specialist equipment; but if you have a top hat and are in possession of a lazy rabbit who is just lying around mooching off you, then why not put them to work? Personally I have yet to master much in the way of magic, but I have learned how to make my money disappear without a trace!

Amateur Theatre

Acting is a perfect pastime for the relentlessly self-obsessed. If you love showing off, kissing co-stars that you don't really like and generally being

a total drama queen this one is definitely for you. Perfect for the frustrated Thespian or would be theatrical costumer. Local amateur theatre is a wonderful place to live out that dream of being on the stage. Even if (like me) all you get to do is play a dancing cardboard box under a giant Christmas tree, you can still tread the boards.

Amateur theatre also offers plenty of opportunities for people who prefer being behind the scenes. Directors, producers, graphic artists, lighting designers and operators, set designers and builders, stand by props people, costumers, sound mixers, stage managers, people to sell tickets and usher in the audience; even fawning fans to pump the star's ego, all of these people are required to pull off a successful production.

Puppetry

Puppetry is the perfect pastime for control freaks and manipulators. Not only do you get to play master of the (puppet) universe, people may well applaud you for your efforts.

Puppetry has been adored by audiences of all ages since as far back as the sixteenth century. The English fairground classic "Punch and Judy", and the traditional Japanese puppet theatre "Bunraku" stand as living testaments to puppetry's timeless appeal. However, in more recent times some rather adventurous Australian gentlemen have turned their private

parts into "puppets", regularly touring the globe with their aptly named show "Puppetry of the Penis"! I kid you not… if you don't believe me, Google it! What's more, they have even trained up a squad of game young gentlemen to perform their lewd form of puppetry at hen's parties. Personally, I don't recommend you try this, it seems like it might be painful and I'm not sure it would go down too well with the relatives.

Leaving aside Australia's somewhat controversial contribution to the art form, putting on a puppet show is a thoroughly engaging creative pursuit that requires all the skills of a full on theatre production. You could try your hand at scriptwriting, directing, or set and costume design. Throw in a bit of ham acting and a few bad jokes and you are up and running. What's more, you can put on a puppet show in a space no bigger than a cardboard box. Why not put on a performance for you local primary school, the local nursing home or even at the grand-kid's birthday party?

There are several types of puppets you can easily make at home, such as finger puppets, glove puppets (like lamb chop), marionettes (like the Thunderbirds), stick puppets (like Kermit), or if you are a bit more ambitious you could even try constructing a full body puppet like the ones used in the Lion King. Of course, you don't have to make or be your own puppet. EBay is teeming with all kinds puppets in all price ranges and budgets.

Stand Up Comedy

Good comedy never gets old. Think of all the amazing comics aged over 50, that slay them in isles. Think John Cleese, Jerry Seinfeld, Wanda Sykes, Whoopi Goldberg, John Stewart, Stephen Colbert, Joe Brand, Alan Davis, Stephen Fry, Phil Jupitus and Sandi Toksvig. Remember the great George Carlin, Phyllis Diler, Lucille Ball and Joan Rivers. Not to mention all the incredible 40 something comics like Tina Fey, Amy Pohler, Margret Cho, Samantha Bee and Chelsea Handler that are showing no signs of slowing down any time soon.

You don't have to have had a long career to try your hand at comedy. If you can make people laugh you will be welcomed just about anywhere. Take the inspiring example of Chuck Esterly. At 89 years of age Chuck decided that he had put his comedy dream on hold long enough, so he took to the stage and performed his very first stand up gig, and he totally crushed it! As soon as his routine hit YouTube it went viral, raking up over half a million views! If you need a bit of extra inspiration to get you motivated, you really should check him out. (Just Google "Chuck Esterly", and you will find him).

Ventriloquism

If your sense of humour is a tad on the harsh side, then what better way to express your antisocial fantasies than delivering a spray of insults under the guise of ventriloquism? If you have a long harboured desire to taunt your friends and family, and have them applaud you for it, ventriloquism is the answer.

Ventriloquism is not just for performers. If you have an unpleasant truth you want to get off your chest, but you lack the courage to come out and say it, why not get your very own "Chucky" doll do the talking for you! No matter how grievous it is, you can get away with saying just about anything with a dummy on your knee!

Clowning Around

Clowning is not just for paedophiles, psychopaths, serial killers, street performers and children's entertainers. Clowning is enduring staple of the circus arts that has been delighting audiences for centuries. After all, where would Cirque du Soleil be without the fire juggling, plate spinning, ball walking, horn blowing, face painting antics of their clowns?

Whether you pay homage to the classic black and white style of Pierrot, the green hair of Herschel Krusty, the dazzling diamonds of Harlequin, the jaundiced robes of Ronald McDonald, the flaming red nose and electrified hair of Bozo, or invent your own original freak faced prankster, donning a clown's persona is a totally liberating process. The moment you get the grease paint on you are not longer playing by the same rules. Once you have your clown face sorted, all you have to do is add a few circus skills to your repertoire and you could be juggling at the local fair or making balloon animals for feral children parties.

Turn Yourself Into Performance Art

Performance art is all about getting out there and doing it. Put a flash mob together and tango through your local shopping mall. You could get an outrageous outfit and turn yourself into a living statue, like one of the living sculptures on the Rambles promenade in the centre of Barcelona.

If your costume is amazing enough you can simply take a seat in a tourist precinct and people will quite literally give you their money. Performance art doesn't have to be formal or structured; it could be anything at all.

The thing about performance art is it requires you to detach yourself from your ego, and any ideas about how you are perceived in the world.

HEDONISTIC

Eat it... Just eat it

Cook with weird implements. Buy a wok or a Moroccan tajine, break out the fondue set or cook your fish in a banana leaf! Fry an egg on your engine! The ways to prepare food are limitless, so why stick with the ones you know.

Bull's Penis

Eat International

Goat curry? Deep-fried crickets? Bull's penis? (Yes I said it). OK, so maybe you don't want the bull's penis, but seriously, there is a world of extraordinary foods out there just waiting for you! Whether it's main courses you have never tried, or desserts you never knew existed the world is a veritable smorgasbord of weird and wonderful tastes and textures. Mix it up, try something you love but done a little bit differently. Instead of potato chips, try sweet potato or taro chips. Go wild with weird chocolate, whether it's chilli chocolate, chocolate coated coffee beans or chocolate covered ants, (yes they do make them). Why not give your regular restaurant a miss and try eating something that you might think is odd. Other than the possibility of food poisoning and death, (which is a risk you actually face whenever you eat anything), what's the worst thing that could happen? I highly recommend you add these international culinary amazements to your bucket list:

Mee Goereng   *Escargot*

Malaysian: Curry laksa, Nasi goereng, Mee Goereng. **Thai:** Pad Thai, Laab, Green curry coconut. **Indian:** Malai kofta, Dahl makani, Palak paneer, Aloo Gobi. **Japanese:** Tempura, Udon, Sushi **French:** Olive Roulade, Escargot, Oursins. **Italian:** Arancini, Angalotti. **Swiss:** Rösti

Rösti   *Dolmades*

(Swiss fried potato, that could be the original hash brown).
Greek: Dolmades, Taramosalata. **Middle Eastern:** Falafel balls, Homos Dip, Baba ganoush. **UK:** Baked beans on toast, Mashed potato, Yorkshire or Black Pudding. **Australian:** Pumkin soup, Vegamite toast (spread thin).

Felafel Balls   *Baked Beans On Toast*

Sweets

Eclaire   *Tiramisu*

Jalebi   *Gulab Jamin*

Italian: Tiramisu, Florentines, Panforte, Cannoli (Ok I know you have tried them already but they really are totally amazing and you should have them again). **French:** Crème brûlée, augnarde, croquembouche, Cachou lajaunie, Fraise tagada, Eclaire. **Indian:** Laddu, Jalebi, Gulab Jamin, Ladoo. **Greek:** Halva, Greek Vanilla. **Mexican:** Chocolate covered coffee beans. **Thai:** Khanom Gluay (Banana Treat) Durian Coconut Milk Soup with Sticky Rice, Banana Leaf Sticky Rice, Fried Banana with Roasted Rice.

If you can't find anything weird and wonderful to excite your tongue locally why not head for somewhere more exotic? Travel to your nearest big city where there are foods from all nations. You could even travel the world on a global gobble fest.

The Cafe Crawl

The cafe crawl is an essential part of life for any cosmopolitan urban sophisticate. Drag your friends to sample and discuss the finer points of Arabica coffee beans, Kona verses Kenya, cappuccino verses a flat white,

espresso verses macchiato; critique the decor, the relative skills (and hipster man bun) of the barista, and generally enjoy the cafe experience. Take your laptop and write that novel while you are there.

The cafe is the perfect environment for socialising with friends, people watching, chatting up strangers, reading a good book, ranting about politics and philosophy, or just generally looking cool and hanging out. However, if you live in a cafe poor area you could always travel to one of the world's great "cafe" cities, Paris, Rome, Vienna, Milan or somewhat surprisingly Melbourne Australia, which has more cafes per head of population than any other city in the world, and has been voted as having the "world's best coffee".

If tea is more your thing you may find a lot of cafes prove disappointing; however a quick trip to the UK and you can travel the country top to bottom while never being more than spitting distance from a phenomenally good tearoom. English tearooms are famous for their scones (no, they not the same as the American ones) with jam (Jelly) and cream, gingham tablecloths and laid back (slow) service.

Drink And Be Merry

It is an indisputable fact that most people love to drink. In some places it borders on a national obsession. The love of alcohol has been with humanity since the very beginning; even our apish cousins are happy to imbibe by gorging themselves on fermenting fruit.

Now, I am not advocating for working oneself into an alcoholic stupor, or hanging out on skid row with a flagon of port in a brown paper bag. (If you are buying your port in flagons, or purchasing your wine in a box you probably should have stopped drinking years ago, or at least converted to mineral water). But, the risk of unchecked alcoholism aside, a good beer, a fine wine and a quality spirit can be a stupendous party starter. There are so many wonderful ways to enjoy the social lubrication of a little tipple.

Wineries And Breweries

In recent years there has been a emerging trend for home brewing and boutique wineries and breweries, (we even have a boutique brewery in our street!). Many of these small operators offer unique products, like organic beer and wine, that you simply cannot get from a mainstream liquor stores. Many of these local breweries sell to local bars and pubs (this is very common in the UK), or open their doors directly to the public. Some have restaurants and cellar doors, and some even offer vineyard tours. There are many vineyards surrounding my city and it is possible to get a bus tour to take you from place to place to sample all the different wines. Many offer "clean skins", which are kind of like the lucky dip of the wine world. They are usually the end bottles from a production run, but what vintage and grape they are is often a mystery. They are often inexpensive to buy but could still be from a very high quality batch; or they could be like quaffing vinegar. It's quite an adventure!

Home Brewing

Craft beer is everywhere these days, and who doesn't love a pint? Home brewing is a great way to get your friends to come and visit. The mere mention of a boutique beer tasting is likely to see a stampede of willing Guinea Pigs (AKA taste testers) at your front door. With starter kits beginning at about $100, home brewing can actually save you money. Of course in most places you are strictly forbidden from selling anything you brew, but there is nothing to stop you brewing up a batch for someone's birthday or for a Christmas present!

Oktoberfest

Break out the pretzels and lederhosen. Everyone should attend an Oktoberfest at least once in their lives. The undisputed king of beer festivals, Oktoberfest is legendary for it's oak barrels, busty serving wenches, oversized tankards and trombone wielding polka bands.

If you cannot get to Germany to enjoy the real deal don't worry; just about every city in the western world gives a nod to the occasion with their very own like named beer and vomit festival. Admittedly some of these copycat Oktoberfest's can be a little tragic, but you will still get to drink lots of beer.

SPORTY

OK, I am going to say this right up front. I am not a sporty person. While I love actively participating in some sports, I think I may have part of my brain missing when it comes to spectating. I genuinely don't understand why some people think the ability to kick a pig's bladder around a field of grass makes someone a hero, nor do I acknowledge that putting a ball in a hoop is something worth doing. And I certainly don't see why someone who is good at such a pointless task should be paid tens of millions of dollars to advertise shoes. I realise that I am in the minority on this and that my profound lack of understanding on these matters leaves me ill equipped to deal with this section of the book; that said, I know some people love sports and I am therefore prepared to have a go at it, but I suspect it won't be pretty.

Go Extreme

Break out the energy drinks and make like a twenty year old. If you like adrenal fatigue and the real possibility of ending up in traction there are plenty of extreme sporting options out there, including abseiling, skydiving, base-jumping, cave diving, wing-suit flying, kite- surfing, paragliding, paint ball, wind surfing and white water rafting. There is an extreme sport for just about every taste and sartorial preference. For example if you long to dress like a toddler but don't want to stand out among your piers skateboarding could be just the thing.

Maybe you like to look a little more formal? If you love the wild adventure of extreme sports but are worried you might be missing out on some of the more domestic joys, why not try extreme ironing?

According to Wikipedia: *"Extreme ironing is both an extreme sport and a performance art in which people take ironing boards to remote locations and iron items of clothing"*.

According to the Extreme Ironing Bureau, extreme ironing is *"the latest danger sport that combines the thrills of an extreme outdoor activity with the satisfaction of a well-pressed shirt."*

Take A Hike

Up hill and down dale, walking is fresh air and nature, (or maybe diesel fumes and car horns if you happen to live on a motorway). But seriously, there are all kinds of walks. Whether you like to hike, dawdle, stride, stroll, saunter, sashay, meander, promenade, ramble, gallivant, traipse, tramp, or schlep around, there is a walk that is just right for you. Whether you are out to show off your sartorial best, or are clad in a parachute fabric sweat suit it doesn't matter.

Wherever you are, there are always fields, mountains, parks, beaches, esplanades and malls to be perambulated. Even if you're feeling a tad constitutionally disabled, shy of a wheelchair you can still get out for a good toddle hurple, limp or shuffle. And if you do happen to be in a wheel chair, then instead of walking you can just let the good times roll.

Lawn Bowls

Long known to be hotbeds of romance and intrigue you should never underestimate the radical nature of the lawn bowls crowd. Believe me, it's not all tea and cakes. While you may never have suspected it, within those starched white skirts and lovingly pressed trousers lurk some of the most outrageous flirts and party people on the planet. Lately some bowls clubs have even opened their doors to the rock and roll crowd. Understanding the truly radical nature of lawn bowlers these degenerate musicians and their entourages have flocked to join their ranks. If you are brave or out there enough to step into the fast lane then lawn bowls could be for you.

Ten-Pin Bowling

When you think about wearing shoes that have been on hundreds of feet before they got to you; when you consider the degenerative health

effects of hot dogs, sodas and other bowling alley food; when your sole aim for the evening is to hurl heavy balls down long alleys in the hope of annihilating the standing order, there is only one inescapable conclusion you can draw. Bowling is the every-man homage to entropy!

However, if you like creating chaos out of order, then you've got to love ten-pin bowling. Personally, I am drawn to anything that involves the catastrophic collision of fast moving balls and stationary objects. I love the sound of the pins crashing to the ground. I love the rise of the triumphant roar when someone scores a strike. I love the teams, the groovy 50's bowling shirts, the cancerous snack foods, it's all totally great. Of course, if you don't want your toes to mingle with the fungi of the masses, you could always buy your own shoes.

Croquet

Croquet may have been popular with the 'in' set back in the 1920's, when everyone was doing the Charleston and dressing like a flapper, but it's made a bit of comeback in recent times.

It's inexpensive, (you can pick up croquet set on EBay for $50-$100). It's gentle on the body, (so you don't need to have stellar strength, stamina or flexibility). You don't even need a manicured lawn. All you need is a rectangle of cut grass and some chalk (or string) to mark out your court. If you don't have the regulation 100 x 50 foot patch it doesn't matter, just adjust the size and shape of the court to fit the available space. For those that might want to get competitive there is even a US croquet association: "http://www.croquetamerica.com".

Take Aim At Archery

Archery is no longer a primitive hunting tool or medieval weapon of war, it is a thoroughly modern sport. It's not just for medievalists, or those that like to play cupid; it's perfect for anyone who enjoys rummaging through the woods searching for stray arrows. Whether you treat it as a hobby, get competitive, or would rather hunt down venison than visit your local butcher, archery is a tremendous; and unlike a lot of other sports, archers

can rise to the top at any age. (American archer Galen Spencer won the gold in a Summer Olympics on his 64th birthday).

There are many different types of archery including traditional archery, target archery, field archery, 3D archery and bow hunting. Traditional archery is your free-range, "Hunger Games" kind of affair. Target archery is fairly self-explanatory; you simply set up a target and shoot arrows at it. Field archery is where you roam through the woods shooting at targets that have been set up along a track. 3D archery is similar to field archery but instead of shooting at targets you shoot at all kinds of foam model animals that have been skilfully hidden throughout the woods, and bow hunting is for those rugged outdoors types that like the visceral gore of killing one's own meat (seriously people, if you're not going to eat it, don't kill it).

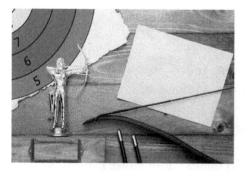

Your choice of bow doesn't just depend on what kind of archery interests you and how strong you are. It is also about how cool you want to look while doing it. Compound bows are good all-rounders, they look impressive and are reasonably easy to use.

Re-curve bows can look a bit geeky, but they are the easiest to handle and require the least physical strength. Long bows look very dramatic but require a lot of grunt, (seriously, it could destroy your shoulder trying to pull one of those things), whereas the crossbow is a hardcore hunting machine and could have you looking as menacing as Rambo on steroids.

Cue Up For Billiards

There are very few activities that are as equally welcomed in a refined English gentleman's club as they are in a Hell's angles hangout; but using long sticks to poke coloured balls around a felted slate table is one of them. The fact that cue sports are accepted by such a broad social spectrum makes them some of the most popular and widely played sports on the planet.

You don't need a body to rival Adonis, you don't even need to be fit; you just need a keen eye and a competitive spirit. If you don't own a table, you can enjoy the social aspect of playing in bars, pubs and clubs. It doesn't matter where you are in the world there will be some kind of pool or billiards competition being held within striking distance, and if you want to go semi pro the only equipment you'll need is a good cue stick. Whether your game is carom, snooker, pool or billiards, the World Pool-Billiard Association (WPA), oversees a huge range of competitions and tournaments. They also have multi-national network of regional affiliates that spans the globe, including the All Africa Pool Association (AAPA), Asian Pocket Billiard Union (APBU), Billiard Congress of America (BCA, Canada and the US), Confederation Panamerica of Billiards (CPB, Latin America and Caribbean), European Pocket Billiard Federation (EPBF, including Russia and the Near East), and last but not least the Oceania Pocket Billiard Association (OPBA, Australia, New Zealand, Pacific islands), so it shouldn't be too hard to find a trophy that's up for grabs somewhere close by.

The WPA and the World Confederation of Billiard Sports have been lobbying hard for cue sports to be included in the Olympics, which is looking increasingly likely. So who knows, if you practice hard enough you might even be able pocket an Olympic gold in your retirement.

Kick On With Martial Arts

While not a traditional pick for a quiet retirement, martial arts are surging in popularity with the over 50's, and not just because they provide a good workout. Martial arts can help you relax, clear the mind, and beat the living cr*p out of any wayward teen that tries a snatch and grab on your wallet.

Martial arts take many different forms, such as Jujitsu, Taekwondo, Karate, Tae-Bo, etc., so it's important that you find the martial art that is right for you. Some of your Bruce Lee, fly through the air kicking and screaming style martial arts can be pretty taxing on the body, but there a number of options that can be practiced to quite an advanced age. Chinese Kung Fu, (which includes forms like "Wing Chun" and "Shaolin Five Animal Style") and the modern Japanese practice of Akido, for example, are both great for older adults. Wing Chung focuses more on speed than raw power, and most of the striking is done open handed, (which is much gentler on the joints and muscles). Akido, which was developed early last century, is a synthesis of a range of martial arts, philosophical and religious beliefs. It was originally created so that practitioners could defend themselves while also protecting their attacker from injury.

Martial arts can be great for strength, cardio and mobility training. Of course, if your body is not used to exercise your muscles are going to get sore and some mild level of pain is to be expected, so take care not to exert yourself to the point of extreme pain. Unless of course you like that kind of thing?

Go Fly A Kite

Suggesting someone "Go fly a kite" may be a polite way to tell an extremely annoying person to disappear, but it's also a mighty fine suggestion for anyone that needs to get out of the house. The first time I flew a kite I was amazed at just how physical and exhilarating it was. You really feel like you are one with the elements, weaving your kite through the wind, pulling, releasing, diving, flying, it's utterly brilliant. Kites can range in price from your simple child's $5 toy right through to professional $1000 models. You can even make your own. There is enormous amount of artistry and creativity on display in individually made kites. Birds, octopus, fish, kittens, insects, dragons, geometric shapes and colours all feature heavily in the kite maker's repertoire.

There is also a great community of kite fliers and festivals out there to explore. For those in the UK you can check out all the best kite festivals on the handy website www.kitecalendar.co.uk or if you are in the USA you might want to check out some of these kite fests. The Huntington Beach Kite Party or the Berkely kite festival in California, the Blossom Kite Festival in Washington DC, Kite Fest Louisiana, the Kids and Kites festival in Chicago, the Great lakes Kite Festival in Michigan, the Wild woods kite festival in New Jersey, the San Francisco kite festival, the summer or fall kite festival in Oregon, the Rogallo kite festival in Nth Carolina or the Washington State International Kite Festival. Wherever you happen to be there are plenty of fun kite festivals out there.

Go Fishing

OK, I get the solitude. I get the fresh air, the meditative, contemplative aspect, but the snaring a sharp hook though a fish's lip seems kind of barbaric. I'm sorry but I just cannot get past the notion that it would really hurt.

Fair enough if you are going to eat it and are prepared to kill it quickly and cleanly once you land it, but this notion of hooking a fish and throwing it back, or skewering live worms on hooks seems kind of like a training activity for psychopaths.

Body Building

If you feel a desperate need to parade around in skimpy Lycra then pumping a bit of iron first might not be a bad idea; after all bulging biceps are not just for twenty-somethings.
There are a plethora of gyms, personal trainers, trophy competitions and websites to help the mature age body builder achieve an insanely cut body.

Contrary to what many people think, body-building is more than just strutting about flexing your muscles. It is a highly disciplined practice that tones up the mind as well as the body. It can improve your focus, determination, mental clarity and self-esteem, as well as your diet, muscle tone and bone density. Be careful though, if you get too strong it could put you on the favours list for any one in need of some heavy lifting.

On Your Bike

While biking can be perfect for greenies, fitness freaks and people without cars it is not without its risks. I don't want to be a Debbie downer here but if you are contemplating getting out on a bike in a city you need to know that biking can be fatal. Sad fact is that people on bicycles are often bullied and ignored by motorists. Cities with bike paths are usually fairly safe, but in most other places you could end up having a nice day out,

or you could end up in traction! If you plan to stray off the bike paths I highly recommend you make your bike as visible as possible by covering it in those fluorescent flags and lighting it up like a Christmas tree! As for appropriate attire, helmets may make you look ridiculous and totally geeky, but they are a necessary evil. And while you don't need those spooky little Lycra shorts with padded bottom, you should wear something BRIGHT BRIGHT BRIGHT, like a high visibility vest or a fluorescent jumpsuit. If you still feel you need something brighter and more noticeable maybe you could entertain the children in passing cars by donning a clown suit? It would definitely make you more of a stand out!

Go Golfing

In this sport of millionaires, vast tracts of highly desirable land are set aside so that the fortunate few can play a rather extravagant form of "ball in a cup". Using long sticks with little wedges at the end golfers attempt to hit a small ball into a cup. The person who does it in the least hits is the winner.

To me golf seems like a long walk for people with short attention spans. You keep hitting the ball to remind yourself which way you are walking. But apparently you can remain competitive to quite an advanced age, which makes golf the perfect sport for mature people that still like to whip the youngsters.

Get On Target With Darts

Whether you want to get seriously competitive or just have bit of fun over a pint of larger, darts is one of the few sports that allows you to have a few drinks, shoot the breeze and practice all at the same time. Which isn't to say

darts isn't a serious sport. The UK's PDC (professional darts corporation) hold a "World Championship" annually in the UK which has a prize fund of £1,500,000, and the winner walks away with £300,000 (approximately US$400,000). Darts also has a good following in the USA.

The National Darts Association, ("www.ndarts.com"), have leagues all over North America, and they hold regular tournaments offering prizes of up to $500,000. If you think you have a chance of hitting the bull's-eye, without taking someone's eye out, why not give it a shot?

Team Sports

Team sports are not for the feint hearted. If you mess up in a solo sport you only have to deal with your own disappointment. Stuff up in a team sport and you have let the entire side down. Conversely, if you win no-one cheers for you personally, they cheer for the team. So you get only, maybe, one tenth of the glory you would on a solo endeavor. It's simple math really. Playing team sports = 10 x the potential down side with only 1/10th of the potential upside. Yes, I know some people love playing basketball, baseball, netball, cricket, soccer, football, polo, hockey, lacrosse and volleyball etc., for the wonderful camaraderie etc., but trust me, with team sports most of the time you only one fumble away from exile!

Target And Clay Shooting

Shooting is another sport where you can remain competitive throughout your life. Senior target shooters are consistently making their way onto the Olympic podium. So if you are going to shoot anything target shooting is definitely the way to go. Targets don't feel it when you pop off a riffle round, or unload a clip into them. And if you want something a bit more challenging clay ducks provide excellent moving targets. Fun with guns, and no one gets hurt! What could be better than that?

Anyone For Tennis?

Never mind the sporty moustaches of the club coaches, the little white player's outfits, or its extraordinary popularity, tennis is the only game in the world where being a total loser gets you love! This fact alone clearly makes tennis one of the best sports ever invented. Animal activists need not be put off either. It's been a very long time since tennis rackets have been strung with catgut, so tennis is now totally Vegan friendly.

LUCRATIVE

Supplement Your Income

While some people love working part-time after they retire, others are forced into it by necessity. But whatever the reason, a small business activity can be a great way to earn a bit extra cash. Everyone knows it can be a bit of a grind trying to carve out a few extra bucks but some methods are easier, and considerably more fun than others.

Have A Yard Sale

Yard sales are a great way to get rid of junk while communing with others in your neighbourhood. You never know who will turn up. When I was younger my mother used to love having yard sales. She loved it so much that she would scour the local trash and treasure markets and car boot sales just to have something to sell. She made some great friendships and she made a pretty penny at it too!

Become A Gold Digger

Marry someone rich for his or her money! Well maybe it's not your first choice in retirement planning but that doesn't mean you have to give up on your gold digging dream; after all, there could be gold in them there hills! Are you in an area where they once found gold? Grab a metal detector and take it for a walk. Old safety pins, tin cans, an old stirrup, there's no telling what you might find.

Airbnb

Air BnB is a website that turns ordinary people's houses into makeshift bed and breakfast accommodation. If you love "meeting new people" Air BnB is not only a wonderful way to have a nose around inside other people's places when you're travelling, but it's a great way to get totally unknown strangers into your home to stay with you.

It's not totally random though, as the website does have a rating system for guests and hosts to rate and reviews their experiences. However, if you just want the money and don't want to interact with a steady stream of random strangers you could have a section of your home converted into a miniature hotel suite, with a private bathroom and cooking facilities, (although realistically if you can afford to do that you probably don't need the money).

Sell Your Opinion

Why not do online surveys?... OK, this really is as dull as watching paint dry, but it requires no real thought or skill and can rake in a small amount of cash. Some online surveys don't pay participants with actual money. Instead companies offer discounts and even free products to people who are willing to give up a little time to answer some questions If you are keen to give online surveys a go then I recommend giving wildly inappropriate answers to spice up this rather dull activity. The wilder and more outrageous the answers the more fun it could be.

Build A Website

We now live in an age of shameless self-promotion and there is no reason you can't be a part of that. Nothing screams "look at me" louder than owning the URL (web address) to your own name, and having a multi page web site to serve as a testament to your limitless brilliance.

www.wix.com is a great place to start for those that have no experience in the dark art of web site construction, although you could save money by starting a site on www.wordpress.com for free (there are plenty of videos on how to do it on Youtube).

But seriously, not all web sites are shameless self-promotion. You can advertise anything, including a charity or an NGO.

Sell Your Handicrafts

While you might enjoy knitting or making clothes and can create things that others would be happy to pay for, the reality is that selling your own handicrafts is a great way to ensure you are paid at the same hourly rate as a third world factory worker. In this age of mass production no one really wants to pay for hand crafted artefacts, so do not, repeat DO NOT do this just for the money. (The only exceptions to this rule are for those marketing geniuses whom are simply brilliant at branding, and mythologising their own work). While you can technically sell your crafts online, or go to local flea markets to display your wares, this is something you should do primarily for FUN FUN FUN (and pocket change). It's true that if your crafts become popular enough, you might find that people will track you down just to buy them (and pay you a good price), but don't go in expecting that. My advice, keep it weird, quirky and above all FUN!

Become An EBay Star

EBay is an excellent way to supplement an income, or just clear out the junk you no longer want. You can sell just about ANYTHING on EBay. As a bet I framed a brown paper bag, and titled it "Concept Art - Brown Paper Bag", and sold it for $35. Admittedly it took a few weeks but it did sell, so the principal is solid. There are lots of other websites, like Craig's List or Gumtree, where you can buy and sell, and the ads are free!

Get A Part-Time Job

This is not serious advice unless you are forced into it by circumstance. The whole point of retirement is that no one is telling you what to do anymore. I know some people like to work, although to my mind getting a part time job defeats the purpose of retirement. If you want a part time job for social interaction or because you just love your work, then OK. But make sure it's on your terms!

Write An E-book And Sell It On Amazon

The fact that you are reading this book right now should provide you with ample evidence that this can be done by someone of limited literary skill, questionable humour and a rather modest intelligence. This alone should be enough to inspire you. There are a few tips and tricks to doing it well, but nothing doctor Google couldn't dig up for you. If you need formatting done "www.upwork.com" is the place. If you want a cheap cover put together try "www.fiverr.com" or "www.upwork.com"

109

Sell From Your Garden

If you are an avid gardener you could turn your talent into a small business? From fruit and vegetables to eggs, compost and cuttings, there is a huge range of stuff from the garden that you can sell or swap. People are always looking to buy quality plants and  produce that are free from industrial chemicals and pesticides. One of my neighbours propagates succulents and sells them from her front porch every weekend. Another man I know has turned his garden into nursery. They both do quite well. I have even heard rumours that there are certain herbs that can be sold for staggeringly large amounts of money, but as yet no one has offered me a princely sum for my basil. Go figure?

Play The Stock Market

Playing the stock market is fun, and can be very profitable but it is really just legitimate gambling; so definitely don't do it with any money you cannot afford to lose. (This is actually good advice!) While the odds are decidedly better than at the casino there are real risks; by all means play but don't bet the farm.

Become A Landlord

If you don't have enough headaches in your life you could try buying some cheap rental property in a questionable neighbourhood and renting it out to drug addicts. This is one of the best ways I know of to add a level of tension and unpredictability to your life without actually leaving the house or doing anything physically dangerous. (Although banging on the door demanding the rent could lead to trouble). If you want to try this exciting pastime make sure you have good insurance.

SPIRITUAL

Explore Your Spiritual Side

Throughout the ages countless parables, myths and stories have been manufactured to explain the inexplicable and imbue our lives with a sense of purpose. Of course, these stories may or may not be true, but what ever "the truth" actually is we still like to think there is something bigger out there than our personal peep-hole into the universe. Musing on what that might be, and which spiritual franchise, if any, has the patent on the real deal is a superb way to fill your days.

Explore The Religions Of The World

Comparative religion is an excellent interest for religious zealots, casual believers, aggressive secularists and the just plain curious. Everyone can get something out of studying the faiths of the world.

Is there a correct religion, and if there is how do you know you were born into it? Maybe there is wisdom in other faiths that would resonate with you. Do you know which major world religions does not believe in god? What exactly do Islam, Christianity and Judaism have in common? Is there any crossover between Hinduism and Buddhism? Why are the Janes extreme pacifists? Why do Sufis like to whirl? How would you know the answer to these questions if you never looked into it? Countless millions have fought and died in the name of their religion, so it's kind of interesting to study what it is that they saw as worth dying for.

Join A Religious Group

If you are totally convinced that your religion is the correct one, or even if you just like a bit of company, why not join a religious congregation. Attending regular religious gatherings is a great way to experience your human connectedness, and possibly avoid eternal damnation in the process.

While there are many fine religious groups that do a lot of selfless community work these groups are by no means your only options. If you simply want to belong to a like-minded community, shun other groups, foster your sense of moral superiority and enjoy the odd bake sale, there

are plenty of religious groups out there that will cater to your needs. If however you are joining a religious group in order to avoid eternal damnation you may ultimately be disappointed, because apparently you have to pick the right denomination of the right religion so God won't be really upset with you. Given how many different brands there are out there your chances of picking the right one are really no better than lottery odds.

Master Meditation

Contrary to conservative opinion meditation is not all navel gazing and OMMing. There are hundreds of different meditation techniques out there, and there is bound to be one that suits you. Did you know the Catholic rosary is a form of meditation? Meditation is like a gymnasium for the mind. It tones up your ability to focus, increases awareness, relaxes the body and generally helps one become more resilient. There are yuppie organisations like TM where you can pay thousands to learn their special brand, or there are free courses provided by some secular groups. There are also many free meditation courses run by Buddhist and Hindu groups.

Flex Out With Yoga

If you didn't get your fill of free love and radical eastern philosophies in the 60's and 70's, you will be thrilled to know that yoga is now totally mainstream. You can now bend and stretch to your hearts content and no-one will accuse you of subverting the dominant cultural paradigm. Apparently yoga can make you stronger and suppler, which can lead to better sex (or so I am told), but please don't let that put you off. If you are not into the whole tantric thing yoga can also provide some excellent rationales for getting all pious and puritanical.

Centre Yourself With Tai Chi

In the west we tend to think of tai chi as being an extremely slow form of oriental exercise, but according to Wikipedia the term "t'ai chi ch'uan" translates as "supreme ultimate fist", "boundless fist", "supreme ultimate boxing" or "great extremes boxing", which all sounds frighteningly macho. In reality tai chi is more like a martial art, a meditation, and an exercise regime all rolled into one; so while it may give you fists that could single-handedly take out an army of street thugs, hopefully it also gives you the self-control not to use them.

The health benefits of tai chi have been praised by thousands of daily practitioners, so why not head to the park for a dawn class?

Commune With Nature

Tree hugging, nudism, mud rolling, skinny-dipping, ice diving, there are so many ways to get in touch with the natural world. You don't need to move to the county; simply walk in the park, plant a tree or go to the water's edge and breathe! Nature is you friend, so don't be a stranger.

CHARITABLE

Volunteer

I am not suggesting volunteering for the French foreign legion, or as a human guinea pig for some sinister medical experimentation. I am talking about social service. Working at homeless shelters, mentoring needy kids, or just generally helping people in your community. There are so many ways to make a difference. You can visit the elderly in hospital or tutor at your local school. Some volunteer work is very social. For example many cities have programs where volunteers help tourists navigate their city. In Auckland, New Zealand there is even a lively group of volunteers that make free cups of tea for people in the arrivals hall at the airport. There is so much joy to be had in helping others, so why not grab a piece of that happiness?

Become A Foster Carer

It is a sad reality that even in first world countries there are a lot of children not getting the love, care and stability they need. There is a desperate need for people who can provide foster care to step in and fill the gap for these kids. If you have a safe home, energy and love to spare this could be an amazing gift to someone in need. My sister had a foster child live with her and her

daughter for a couple of years and it was a great experience for my niece, (who is an only child). Most jurisdictions offer some level of financial support for carers who take in needy children, so even you are not flush it may still be an option.

Help Out With Animal Rescue

Becoming an animal rescuer is a wonderfully rewarding thing to do. Whether you take in injured wildlife or needy domestic animals, the love and care you give can literally save lives. If you cannot take on a pet full time there are many charities and services that will provide you with food and veterinary care while they either search for a permanent home for the animal, or rehabilitate it for re-release back into the wild. This can be a tremendous way for someone who is unable to take on a pet for life to get the joy and benefits of caring for another living creature.

Feed The Homeless

You can volunteer at a shelter or registered charity, or you can just go out and do it. You will be pleased to know that some of the proceeds of this book go to feed the homeless. But I must confess, I don't do this just because I am a lovely person (which of course, I am). It's actually a totally selfish act! Feeding homeless people is one of the most amazingly feel good things I have ever done. I fill my shopping trolley with sandwiches, fruit and bottled water and head off into the city. My husband and I walk the streets offering food and drink to any homeless people we see. For the $40 it takes to stock the cart, I can get far more joy, satisfaction and purpose that any cinema, show or fancy restaurant meal has ever bought me.

For anyone who is scared by this concept, please don't be. In my experience most homeless people have suffered some kind of trauma or misfortune, which has lead to job loss, addiction, and in some cases depression or mental illness; but the smiles that come to suffering people's faces when you stop and talk to them, ask them their stories, and show them some kindness, are some of the deepest, most profound smiles I have ever seen. If you have never done this, then I highly recommend it. It can put your life squarely into perspective.

Hold A Charity Gala

If you like your social work with a little more celebrity glam, why not try high-end fundraising. There are plenty of rich folk out there who would never get their hands dirty at the coalface of social service, but would happily spend thousands on a plate at a charity gala.

Learn To Love Other People

OK, we are not talking about the "swinging" kind of love here, (although if you really want to and your partner is up for it then more power to you); we are talking agape, fraternity, sorority and love for our fellow humans. Everyone knows that humanity can be pretty dreadful. There are so many annoying, selfish, stupid people out there. That's why loving humanity is such a great challenge to take on. It's like climbing Everest. There are so many obstacles to overcome, but once you get there you will be on top of the world.

The fact is, tolerance, compassion, empathy, kindness, generosity and patience serve their possessor far more than their recipient, so why not give it a go? Even if you still have well founded doubts and suspicions about other people, you can still learn to love them and treat them with kindness.

NOMADIC

Hit The Road

Let the spirit of Willie Nelson wash over you. The anonymity, the appallingly bad gas station food, the curious cast of characters that pop up along the way; road trips are a magical kind of freedom. They even have their own movie genre. Whether you have a caravan or camper, or just a car, everyone knows roads are simply begging to be hit, and who better to hit them than you?

Take A Day Trip

Admittedly taking a trip doesn't mean quite what it did in the 60's and 70's, but that doesn't mean it can't still be fun. Unless you live in Antarctica or the wilds of Siberia there is probably something totally fabulous within a days drive of where you are now.

Caravans And RV's

If you love clogging up traffic on small country roads and staying in trailer parks, McDonald's car parks and friend's driveways, then caravans and RV's are definitely for you!

There is a level of comfort and predictability to traveling with your own hotel room in tow. You can potter at your own pace, or join convoy with other RV enthusiasts. Why not take a caravan to Burning Man or Glastonbury? Go on a spiritual pilgrimage to see all the

"LARGE" things. (I am particularly keen to see the world's largest shrimp) Caravans and RV's are perfect for people who need regular rest stops, or simply like to go at their own pace. As an added bonus you can stop whenever you like and bid a hasty exit when the locals prove to be agonizingly boring.

Guided Tours

Whether it is one of those tourist buses that circles most cities, a walking tour of the local sites, a bus ride past the houses of celebrities or a guided tour through a gallery, winery, museum, historical village, or even a film studio, short day tours are everywhere. They are usually easy on the pocket, not too taxing on the schedule and are a fantastic way to explore wherever you happen to be. Usually the guides are a wealth of intriguing information that you just wouldn't get if you simply poked around on your own.

Take A Cruise

If you love Hawaiian shirts, straw hats, chlorine pools, playing quoits, nerdy bands and endless smorgasbords full of average cold cuts, then cruising is definitely for you. On the downside, if there are any fellow cruisers that are so excruciatingly boring that they make you want to jump overboard, you will be stuck with them for the duration. Don't be overly

discouraged though, even with the most persistently annoying of co-passengers you should still be able to find a spot on deck where you can enjoy the solitude of staring silently out across the crystal waters, (at the very you least you should be able to lose them when you are in port).

Join The Jet Set

Air travel has never been cheaper. These days you can get just about anywhere without breaking the bank. And there are all kinds of weird and wonderful deals from the airlines; like around the world tickets, where you can have a set number of stops but you have to keep

flying in the same direction. Then there is the much loved mystery flight, where you book a return flight at the airport and they put you on the first seat that comes up regardless of where it is going. But commercial airlines are far from the only way to fly. You could book a jaunt in a charter plane, a glider, a helicopter or even a seaplane.

Package Tours

If you always hated colouring outside the lines a package tour might be just right for you. If you love the security and comfort of travelling with a group, having a well-defined budget and a predetermined itinerary and activity schedule, a package tour can take all the worry out of planning your trip. A good travel package should include your transportation, guided tour groups, and accommodation and breakfasts. While you can always make friends with other people on the same package, you could also get your own group together.

Up Up And Away

Hot air ballooning is an extraordinary experience. It's not just the sense of being so high up in an open basket, it's the sound of the wind, the absence of the engine, and of course it is all about the champagne and strawberries as you float across the skies.

Explore Your Own Backyard

Why not try being a tourist in your town or city? Pull on those travel slacks; sling your camera around your neck and step outside your own front door. Many people live in a place their whole lives without ever realizing all of the magic that is right under their noses.

It's human nature to take things that are at hand for granted, but in so doing you can miss out on the fun and adventure that is right there for the taking. If you are really scratching for a local destination try checking out the local tourist bureau. They will have a wealth of information about what's on offer; and will probably be able to point you to amazing things that you never knew were there.

See The World!

Everyone knows that their country is the best and every other country in the world is doing it wrong. The fact is, other countries just don't understand how things ought to be done and clearly they need people to go over there and set them straight. Missionaries and world travellers have been doing this for centuries, so why not join them?

Be amazed by how people from other lands have no understanding or sympathy for your special brand of culture. Vent your anger at locals who don't understand you when you speak slowly and loudly at them in your own language. Offend countless people by having no understanding of what is acceptable in their culture.

But seriously, world travel is an excellent way to broaden your horizons, and step outside your own culture. Experience things from a different perspective, like the view from on top of an elephant, or the giddy heights of Machu Picchu. Take a trip on the Orient Express, wander the Silk Road, ride a camel across the desert. Apart from the all unfamiliar sights, sounds and smells there is a world full of people out there just ready to make new friends.

You can find special travel packages that will take you from the east to the west, and the north to the south. There really are no limits to where you can go, so why not see it all?

THE LIFE AQUATIC

Since the dawn of time humanity has had a fascination with water. Most of the world's surface is water. Most of our bodies are made up of water. Without water we simply could not survive. Since before recorded history we have been taking to the sea for food, for travel and for the sheer pleasure of it, so get out there.

Snorkelling

This is a great pastime for those that prefer to swim with the fish rather than catch them. Apparently there are over three million shipwrecks on the ocean floor, not to mention some extraordinary coral reefs. While snorkelling can be done in the shallows for next to nothing, deep sea diving is not a cheap exercise. However, if you don't mind the possibility of coming nose to nose with a shark, or breathing tank air then this activity could be for you.

Deep sea diving requires a lot of expensive equipment and it all needs to be kept in top order, so it is probably better to take some classes to see if it is really for you before you splash out on a kit. There are many diving schools held in local swimming pools where you can learn the basic diving skills without spending a fortune or risking life and limb. That said, deep sea diving has a reputation for being one of the most incredible experiences there is. What better way to while away the days than to get your wetsuit on and explore the ocean floor.

Boating

Once the purview of the mega rich, anyone of modest means can now enjoy a day on the water. Admittedly it might be in a tiny little dinghy or a rusty old sail boat, but a day on the water is a day on the water. If you are really desperate to get out there you could even catch a ferry. Many cities and towns have modestly  priced ferries as part of their public transport system. What better way to see New York from the water on a shoestring?

Get In The Swim

 Swimming is so much more than a great way to cool down on a hot day. Whether you go jump in the lake, dive into a swimming pool, hit the waves at the beach, or splash out in a dam or river, swimming is a great stress reliever. It is also one of the best exercises for anyone over 40. It builds endurance, increases cardiovascular fitness, tones your muscles, builds strength and helps in maintaining a healthy body weight; all while taking the impact stress off your body. Swimming is pretty well everything you could want in workout. It's the perfect exercise for anyone with any kind of muscular skeletal problem arthritis, bad back or asthma.

Dive Right In

If you live near a swim centre with a diving pool then you are in luck. High diving is quite possibly the most thrilling, most exhilarating experiences you can have for pocket change. Most pools will let you dive over and over again for the price of a single entry ticket. The best thing is, diving is really very low risk, especially for something that can give you such a surge of adrenalin. Even if you are not quite up to jumping off the high tower, you can still get quite a rush hurling yourself off the lower levels.

Water Polo

If you enjoy all the health benefits of swimming, but would prefer something a bit more competitive and social, why not check and see if your local swimming centre has a water polo team that is suitable for you. If they don't, and the idea appeals, why not start one?

Workout In The Water

Aquarobics classes are the perfect place to show off your skirted swimsuit and floral bathing cap. Yes, there will be some annoyingly over enthusiastic 20 year old with a ghetto blaster bouncing up and down poolside, yelling at you to move it, but you can ignore her.

It's the perfect exercise for those with a little more girth or those that simply prefer to float through their exercises. Chances are you will find water aerobics classes at your local swimming pool.

Paddle Your Own Canoe

The combined forces of evolution and human ingenuity have been hard at work on the hollow log. So much so that these days there are a whole range of floating, paddling sports to indulge in. Whether you fancy the relative

solitude of canoeing and kayaking, the highly honed team co-ordination of a six person rowing team, or just paddling round the lake in a giant floating bicycle, it's a great way to get fit and enjoy the sunshine of the day. Of course, if you prefer to sit back and let someone else do all the hard work for you, a trip to Venice for a ride in a gondola might be in order.

TECHNICAL

I realise that most people already know their way around a computer, and if you are reading this as an e-book you could probably just skip ahead now. But if you are a committed Luddite now is the time to seriously get over it.

Get Online

No matter what you are interested in the Internet will help you do it faster, cheaper and better. And it's not just the boring mundane stuff like doing your banking, paying your bills and ordering your grocery shop. You can get in touch with others who share your interests, find cheap hotels, cheap airfares, bargain wines, art supplies, obscure music and literature, the latest advances in kayaks, gardening tips, special interest clubs, online dating, in fact you can find just about anything you can think of on the net. I even found a husband!

Refusing to use a computer is like refusing to learn to read. Sure you can have a life without reading, but that life is not going to be as rich, and everything you do is going to be far more difficult. If you cannot find someone in your sphere who can help you get on line then most towns have some kind of free classes available, so check with your local library, council or shire for what is available in your area.

Write An App. Or A Computer Program

Apparently it is not that hard to do. The Internet is full of instructions and programs to help you do it. It could be a game, a recipe builder, a scrapbook maker, a heart rate monitor, an app. that orders your breakfast at the local cafe, or even an app. to tell you when a Mormon missionary is approaching your door so you can get the tea and cakes ready; it could be anything at all.

Build A Robot Or An Electronic Gizwaz

You can get all kinds of kits from your local electronics store, or design your own. There are countless electronic projects you can throw together.

Contrary to what you may think amateur electronics is not just for 15 year-olds. I know a man who actually retired on the proceeds of a foot pedal he designed. You can build your own doorbell, graphic equalizer, synthesizer, maybe even a robot slave to do your bidding?

FAMILY ORIENTED

I admit that this may or may not be a bonus depending on the nature of your family. If your family is populated by violent, anti social criminals you might want to give it a miss, but if your family is all warm fuzzy bear hugs and endless camp fire sing-alongs then by all means enjoy.

See More Of Your Siblings

No one understands the unique madness you had to endure growing up better than your siblings. No one will ever get your jokes, quirks and idiosyncrasies quite like they do. They have known you throughout the best and the worst of your life. They know the setbacks you have suffered, and the victories you have won. Unfortunately, sometimes the pressures of your own family, the tyranny of distance, or even long unresolved conflict can lead to us losing touch with our brothers and sisters. Now is the time to reconnect. While it may not always work out the way we want it to, reconnecting with long lost, or rarely seen family is always worth a try. You could be pleasantly surprised.

Hang Out With Your Grand-kids

Do you enjoy visits from your grandchildren, or are they a bit whiny and demanding? The next time your kids dump their kids on you why not get your own back by teaching the little darlings the finer points of mud pie making, finger painting, clay modelling or anything else that will get them totally caked in muck for the car ride home. Give them a festival of filth and they will just love coming to see you!

Of course if they are a bit more computer game oriented why not join them in wasting their lives. Online worlds like "World of Warcraft" for example can eat up years of valuable time you could otherwise spend actually living.

OUR FAMILY TREE

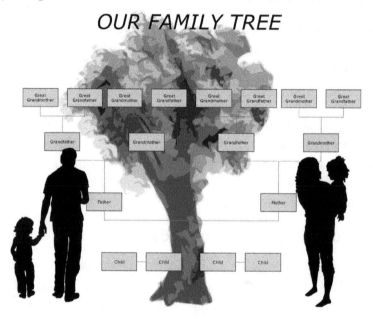

Genealogy And Ancestry

No need to limit your family interaction just to the currently living. Why not have a nose around the family tree? Who knows, go back far enough and your sleuthing may turn up some unexpected royalty, some toffee nosed aristocracy or maybe even a coal miner. Ancestry can get quite addictive, so it's good to know that you don't have to restrict yourself to your immediate family. If you get the bug there is nothing to stop you tracking back the ancestral lines of your friend's families, your siblings or children's partners, or even the deep dark family past of a favourite celebrity.

A Quick Word In Closing

The world is full of strange and wonderful octopus, bats, spiders, frogs, gnats, elephants, ant eaters, mosquitoes, chickens, pheasants, turkeys, donkeys, horses, zebras, dogs, wolves, tree ferns, daisies, periwinkles, mice, impala, ladybugs, flies, moths, shrews, moles, slow worms, snakes, eels, sharks, whales, dolphins, fish, corals, muscles, clams, crocodiles, alligators etc., and somehow you managed to be lucky enough to be born human. Blessed with a critical thinking brain, opposable thumbs and an endless range of possibilities we humans should not squander the great gift we have been given.

Life is short, and may or may not have any meaning beyond the meaning we give it. The one thing we can do to truly honour this life is to live it to the fullest for as many days as we are able.

Be as kind and patient as you can be with others. Be relentless in your quest for a fully actualized life! Enjoy the freedoms you have, for they are but the blink of an eye.

Seize your day, and laugh heartily!

Cheers Stella

Resources

There are literally countless resources out there, many of them totally free. It is the joy of the digital age that you can learn just about anything, find just about anyone or go just about anywhere, and do it all more cheaply and easily than at any other time in human history.

You can use websites like www.meetup.com to find people, groups or clubs in your local area that share you interests, or you could take up a FREE online course. While I have barely scratched the surface of what is available I want to offer you this list of FREE (well most of them should be) courses and resources. This list is by no means comprehensive, but it should give you some idea of the breadth and scope what is out there and available to anyone with access to a computer.

General Academic Courses
www.edx.org
http://www.openculture.com/freeonlinecourses
http://oedb.org/open/
www.coursera.org
www.extension.harvard.edu/open-learning-initiative
General Writing Courses
https://www.class-central.com/report/writing-free-online-courses/
http://www.creative-writing-now.com/free-online-writing-courses.html
http://bubblecow.com/free-online-writing-courses
http://bit.ly/29mbTg8
www.futurelearn.com/courses/start-writing- fiction

General Music Courses
www.edx.org/school/berkleex
www.springboard.com/blog/30-best-free-online-music-courses/
http://www.berkleeshares.com/
http://www.earmaster.com/music-theory-online/course-introduction. html
https://alison.com/learn/music
http://www.open.edu/openlearn/history-the-arts/culture/music
http://study.com/articles/10_Sources_for_Free_Online_Music_ Courses.html

Piano Courses

http://www.pianonanny.com/

https://www.hoffmanacademy.com/

http://www.zebrakeys.com/

https://www.youtube.com/watch?v=ggIDo2Fsv48

http://www.gopiano.com/

http://www.learnpianoonline.com/

http://www.true-piano-lessons.com/free-piano-lessons.html

Guitar Courses

http://www.guitarlessons.com/guitar-lessons/

http://www.justinguitar.com/

https://www.guitartricks.com/

http://www.theguitarsuite.com/

http://guitarcompass.com/free-lessons/

http://www.tabs4acoustic.com/en/

Screenwriting Courses and Resources

http://www.bbc.co.uk/writersroom/opportunities/introduction-to-Screenwriting

http://www.my ik.com/FilmSchool/screenwriting.html

https://www.lights lmschool.com/blog/free-screenwriting-courses/

http://www.scriptmag.com/free/

http://www.filminquiry.com/10-mostly-free-online-courses- filmmaking/

Journalism Courses

http://study.com/articles/List_of_Free_Online_Journalism_Classes_ and_ Courses.html

http://www.mulinblog.com/mulinblog-online-j-school-course-schedule/

http://www.onlinecollege.org/2009/05/20/skip-journalism-school-50- free-open-courses/

http://journalismdegree.org/2009/top-50-free-open-courseware-classes- for-journalists/

Photography Courses

https://www.creativelive.com/photography

https://www.udemy.com/draft/23338/

http://petapixel.com/2014/07/03/best-free-online-photography- courses-

tutorials/
http://freephotocourse.com/online-photography-course.html
http://digitalphotobuzz.com/6-totally-free-online-photography-classes

Gardening Courses
http://www.openlearningworld.com/innerpages/Vegetable%20
Gardening.htm
https://www.greenwoodnursery.com/free-online-gardening-courses
http://www.organicauthority.com/organic-gardening/top-5-online-
gardening-courses.html
http://www.freestudentcourses.co.uk/gardening/
http://www.bbc.co.uk/learning/subjects/gardening.shtml

Stained Glass Courses
https://www.youtube.com/watch?v=EZL1ktDPt0g
https://www.youtube.com/watch?v=E0xACBQa4UQ&list=PLEA6731
D93C734AB2

Carpentry Courses
http://study.com/articles/List_of_Free_Online_Carpentry_Courses_ Classes_
and_Learning_Materials.html
http://www.thewoodwhisperer.com/

Meditation Courses
http://meditation.org.au/online.asp
http://aromeditation.org/
http://web.horde.org/terms/Free_Online_Mediation_Training_Course
http://marc.ucla.edu/body.cfm?id=22

Yoga Courses
https://alison.com/learn/yoga
http://www.yogadownload.com/free-online-yoga-classes.aspx
http://www.popsugar.com/fitness/Websites-Offer-Free-Yoga-
Classes-21156881

INDEX

INDEX

INDEX

CPSIA information can be obtained
at www.ICGtesting.com
Printed in the USA
LVHW051212250621
691135LV00008B/517